PROGRESSIVE

Complete
Learn To Play
DRUMS
Manual

by
Craig Lauritsen

Visit our Website
www.learntoplaymusic.com

The Progressive Series of Music Instruction Books, CDs, and DVDs

Published by
KOALA MUSIC
PUBLICATIONS

PROGRESSIVE COMPLETE LEARN TO PLAY DRUMS
I.S.B.N. 978 1 86469 258 7
Order Code: CP-69258
Acknowledgments
Cover Photograph: Phil Martin
Photographs: Phil Martin

For more information on this series contact;
LTP PublicationsPty Ltd
email: info@learntoplaymusic.com
or visit our website;
www.learntoplaymusic.com

CONTENTS

4

CONTENTS CONTINUED

INTRODUCTION

This book presumes no previous musical experience and clearly and carefully familiarises the reader with the theoretical and practical knowledge required by the performing drummer.

Rhythmic knowledge, understanding and execution is vital to all musicians and in particular drummers. Therefore, rhythmic figures are introduced in a carefully graded progressive format, beginning with easily digestible 1 bar phrases, followed by 16 bar sight reading exercises, and finally, exploring the practical application on drumkit of each rhythmic figure.

The book features 31 sight reading exercises, 37 solos in various musical styles, 42 rudiments, numerous drum fills, information on the development of 4 way independence, how to practice, counting systems, linear patterns, polyrhythms, advanced independence, jazz independence, ostinato patterns, drum tuning, maintenance and more.

The guidance of an experienced teacher who encourages and inspires you to learn, is invaluable.

Remember two things:
1. Anything is achievable.
2. Have fun, because that's really what it's all about.

Other books also available from the author:
Progressive Drum Method
Progressive Drum Grooves
1,000,000 Drum Grooves
Progressive Rhythm Section Method
Progressive Rhythm Section Grooves
Progressive Blues Drumming
Progressive Country Drumming

USING THE COMPACT DISCS

This book comes with **two compact discs** which demonstrate almost all the examples in the book. The recording lets you hear how each example should sound. Practice the example slowly at first, gradually increasing the tempo. Once you are confident you can play the example evenly without stopping the beat, try playing along with the recording. You will hear a hi-hat click at the beginning of each example, to lead you into the example and to help you keep time. A small diagram of a compact disc with a number as shown below indicates a recorded example.

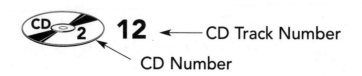

CD 2 **12** ← CD Track Number

CD Number

EXPLANATION OF NOTATION

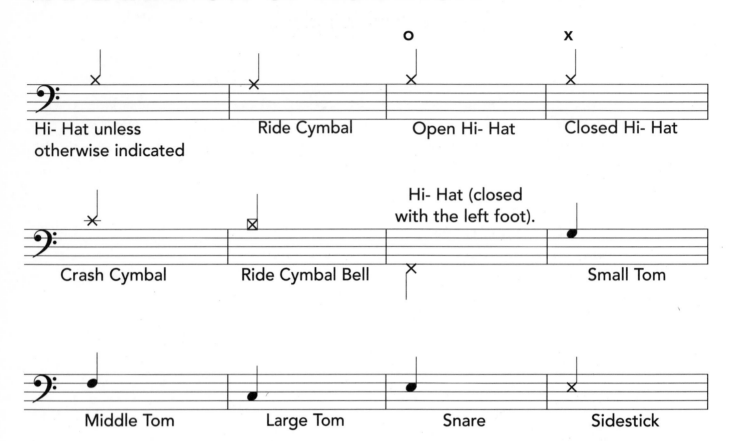

Hi- Hat unless otherwise indicated
Ride Cymbal
Open Hi- Hat
Closed Hi- Hat

Crash Cymbal
Ride Cymbal Bell
Hi- Hat (closed with the left foot).
Small Tom

Middle Tom
Large Tom
Snare
Sidestick

Bass Drum
Accent
(Play the note louder)

Sidestick

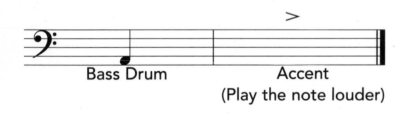
cresc. - Gradually increased volume

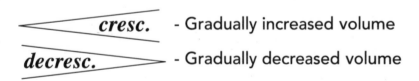
decresc. - Gradually decreased volume

RH = Right Hand   **RF = Right Foot**
LH = Left Hand   **LF = Left Foot**

NOTE:
The Right hand is presumed playing all ride cymbal, ride cymbal bell, hi-hat, crash and cowbell parts. The left hand is presumed playing all snare drum hits. Any sticking change will be indicated.

EQUIPMENT

PARTS OF THE DRUM KIT

PARTS OF THE DRUM STICK

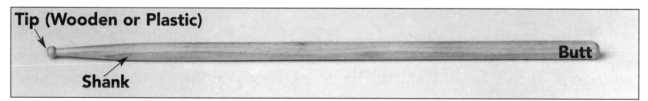

PARTS OF THE DRUM

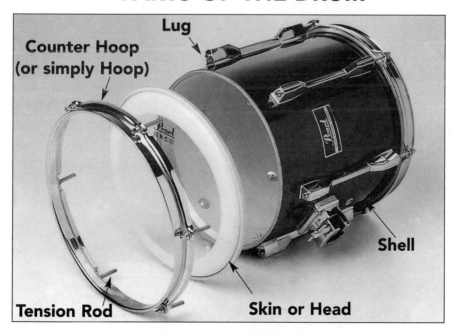

HOLDING THE DRUM STICKS

There are two accepted ways of holding the sticks. They are:

1) **The Traditional Grip** (Photo 1)
2) **The Matched Grip** (Photo 2)

Traditional Grip

Matched Grip

THE TRADITIONAL GRIP

The left hand stick is held at the very base of the thumb, between the thumb and the knuckle of the first finger. This point becomes the fulcrum or pivoting point of the stick. The stick then rests between the second and third fingers, two on top of the stick and two underneath the stick.

The right hand fulcrum is between the thumb and the first joint of the first finger, with the remaining fingers wrapped lightly around the stick. It is important to keep the two fingers of the left hand on top of the stick and the remaining fingers of the right hand in light contact with the bottom of the stick, as the fingers will later be used to increase stick speed.

THE MATCHED GRIP

The right and left hand hold the sticks in exactly the same way as the right hand in the traditional grip method.

It is entirely up to you to use the grip that feels the most comfortable to you. However, I personally recommend the matched grip method because a greater reach and a greater volume level are achievable using this grip.

3 STEPS TO STICK CONTROL

1) *Find the BALANCE POINT of the stick -*

The point at which the stick is held should also be the balance point of the stick, the balance point meaning how far along the stick you should place your grip so that the maximum response is gained from the stick. This point can be found by placing the stick over the first finger and dropping the stick onto a practice pad or snare drum (see photo). The greater the number of natural bounces the stick makes, the closer you are to finding the balance point. The balance point occurs roughly 1/3 of the way up the stick (from the butt end).

2) *Relax the grip -*

It is important to relax your hold on the stick, as too much pressure will 'choke' the stick. The more relaxed the grip, the more easily the stick can pivot within the fulcrum. This leads to a better sound, greater endurance and greater speed.

3) *Keep the stick height uniform -*

If the height of each individual stroke and the height between the two sticks is the same, the resulting sound will be even and constant.

If you follow these three rules when practicing, your stick control should develop quickly. The best way to obtain speed is to always remain relaxed, and to practice precisely.

NOTE VALUES

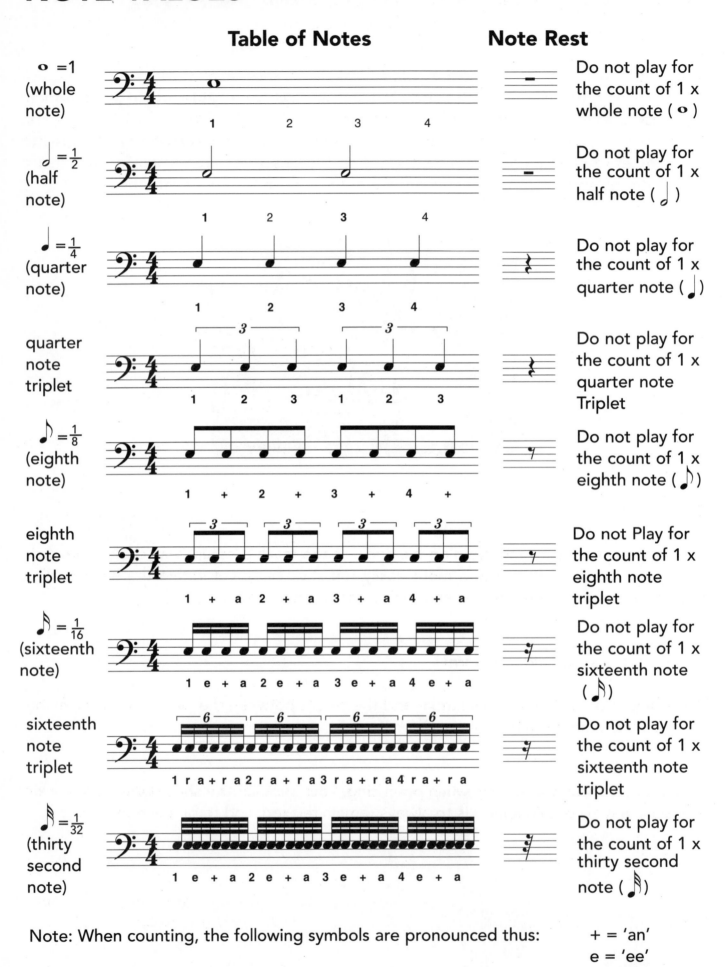

Table of Notes **Note Rest**

o =1
(whole note) — Do not play for the count of 1 x whole note (**o**)

♩ =½
(half note) — Do not play for the count of 1 x half note (**♩**)

♩ =¼
(quarter note) — Do not play for the count of 1 x quarter note (**♩**)

quarter note triplet — Do not play for the count of 1 x quarter note Triplet

♪ =⅛
(eighth note) — Do not play for the count of 1 x eighth note (**♪**)

eighth note triplet — Do not Play for the count of 1 x eighth note triplet

♬ =1/16
(sixteenth note) — Do not play for the count of 1 x sixteenth note (**♬**)

sixteenth note triplet — Do not play for the count of 1 x sixteenth note triplet

♬ =1/32
(thirty second note) — Do not play for the count of 1 x thirty second note (**♬**)

Note: When counting, the following symbols are pronounced thus:

+ = 'an'
e = 'ee'
a = 'uh'
r = 'er'

UNDERSTANDING NOTE VALUES

The table of notes shows every note type you are likely to encounter, with the corresponding rests for each in the next column (note Rests). Here are a few points to help you understand note values:

1. Tempo (beats per minute) dictates the speed of a piece of music. If the tempo is ♩ = 60, one quarter note is being played every second. If the time signature is $\frac{4}{4}$, the information contained within one bar must run for the same duration as four quarter notes (or four seconds). Any note type(s) can be used within the bar. Therefore, note values are like fractions, dividing the amount of notes being played over a specific time period into different amounts. At a fixed tempo, the greater the number of notes per bar, the greater the speed at which they are played.

2. In $\frac{4}{4}$ time, the digits 1-4 and the sounds **e, + , a , r** are used when counting, to signify fractional divisions of the bar.

3. Wherever possible, notes are grouped together to make reading easier e.g. sixteenth notes are grouped together in fours rather than written individually.

THE METRONOME

A Metronome is a mechanical or electronic device that emits a sound to indicate a specific tempo. The tempo (beats per minute) is adjustable.

The metronome has four functions:

1. It allows you to find an exact tempo.

2. It acts as a control for your timing so that you don't rush or slow down during your playing.

3. It indicates improvements which might otherwise go unnoticed.

4. It shows you the level and boundaries of your technique.

Using the metronome:

1. Set the metronome at a comfortable tempo and play the specific exercise through 20 times.

2. Reset the metronome 4-8 beats faster and again play the exercise 20 times.

3. Repeat this process until you reach a tempo where you begin to struggle and tense up. Reset the metronome 4-8 beats slower and again play the exercise 20 times.

4. Whenever you feel tense repeat step 3. Remember, the way to achieve speed is to remain relaxed and practice precisely. Practicing when you're tense will only teach you how to be tense, and in the long term may cause physical damage.

RUDIMENTS OF MUSIC

Music is written on a **staff**, which consists of five parallel lines between which there are four spaces.

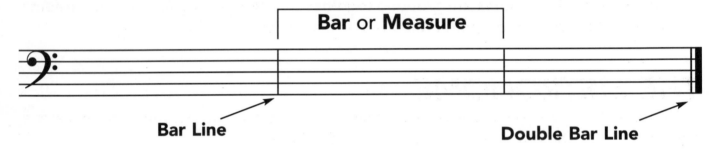

MUSIC STAFF —— Staff Line

All of the individual parts of the drum kit are written on different lines or spaces. (See explanation of notation page 6).

Bar Lines are drawn across the staff, to divide the music into sections called **bars** or **measures**. Bars are used to break the music into smaller digestible parts, much like spaces between words.
A **double bar line** signifies either the end of the music, or the end of an important section of it.

Bar or **Measure**

Bar Line   Double Bar Line

TIME SIGNATURES

At the beginning of each piece of music, after the bass clef, is the **time signature** e.g.

The **time signature** indicates the number of beats per bar (the top number) and the type of note receiving one beat (the bottom number).

4 - This indicates 4 beats per bar.
4 - This indicates that each beat is worth a quarter note.

$\frac{4}{4}$ is the most common time signature used and is sometimes represented by this **C** symbol called Common Time.

TEMPO

Tempo indicates the speed of a piece of music and is measured in **beats per minute.**
e.g. ♩ = 60 would indicate that each quarter note has a duration of 1 second.

REPEAT SIGNS

There are four symbols in common usage which are used to indicate that a portion of music is to be repeated.

1. Two dots placed before a double bar line indicate that the music is to be repeated, from the beginning of the piece of music or from a previous set of repeat signs.

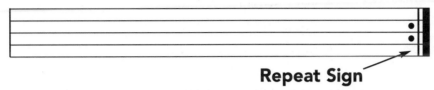

Repeat Sign

2. The following indicates that the previous bar only is to be repeated.

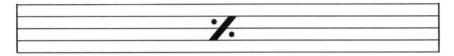

3. The number 2 placed over a bar line crossed with two dotted diagonal lines, indicates that the previous two bars are to be repeated.

4. Diagonal lines are used to indicate that a quarter note length (1 beat) of information per diagonal line be repeated from the same position in the previous bar. These are used so that fills or accents of less than four quarter notes in length can be easily added to repeated rhythms e.g.

is equal to:

FIRST AND SECOND TIME BARS

Play through [1._____ the first time, then skip to [2._____ on the repeat.

DYNAMICS

Dynamics are the varying degrees of volume of sound. Using dynamics when playing creates interest and excitement, and hence mastery of dynamics is vital to all musicians.

There are 3 commonly used symbols which describe levels of volume:

p	= pianissimo	= very softly
m	= mezzo	= moderate or medium
f	= forte	= loudly, with strength

These symbols can be combined to indicate many different levels of volume, for example:

ppp	= as quietly as possible
mp	= moderately quiet
mf	= moderately loud (normal playing level)
fff	= as loud as possible

There are 2 symbols to indicate gradual volume changes:

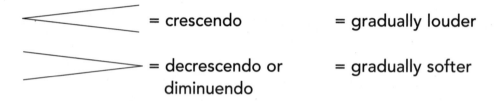

= crescendo = gradually louder

= decrescendo or diminuendo = gradually softer

Below are some exercises designed to help you develop control over many volume levels.

Practice all rudiments, reading exercises and drum patterns with the following dynamic variations:

(a) *ppp*

(b) *mf*

(c) *fff*

(d) *ppp* ———— *fff* ————— *ppp*

(e) *fff* ————— *ppp* ———— *fff*

(f) Choose some dynamic levels of your own to change between.

Practice exercises over varying lengths, with varying tempos. Always use a metronome.

With drum patterns of your choice, practice changing the dynamics of one or more limbs without affecting the volume of any other limb. Use the dynamic variations (a) - (f) above.

For example:

Whilst playing a rock pattern, change the dynamic level of only the bass drum without changing the volume of the hi-hat or snare.

SECTION 1

THE QUARTER NOTE

This is a quarter note worth one count. There are **four** quarter notes in one bar of ⁴⁄₄ time.

Count: 1 2 3 4

In ⁴⁄₄ time, quarter notes divide the bar into four evenly spaced hits. If the tempo is ♩ = 60, each bar of ⁴⁄₄ time has a duration of four seconds. Each quarter note hit has a duration of **one second.**

Example 1 is played at sixty beats per minute to illustrate the paragraph above. The right and left hand alternate on the snare drum, This is called a **single stroke roll** or **alternating sticking.**

1.

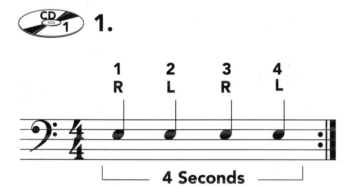

THE QUARTER NOTE REST

This is a quarter note rest and indicates one beat of silence. Quarter note rests are counted but no hit is played for that beat.

COUNTING

It is important to count, preferably aloud.
Counting has the following advantages:

1) It helps to reinforce a consistent metronomic pulse.

2) It helps you understand and keep track of rhythmic events.

3) It aids your memory retention.

4) It improves your level of concentration.

16

1 bar rhythmic variations featuring the rhythmic figures ♩ and 𝄽.
There are **sixteen** rhythmic possibilities using quarter notes and quarter note rests.

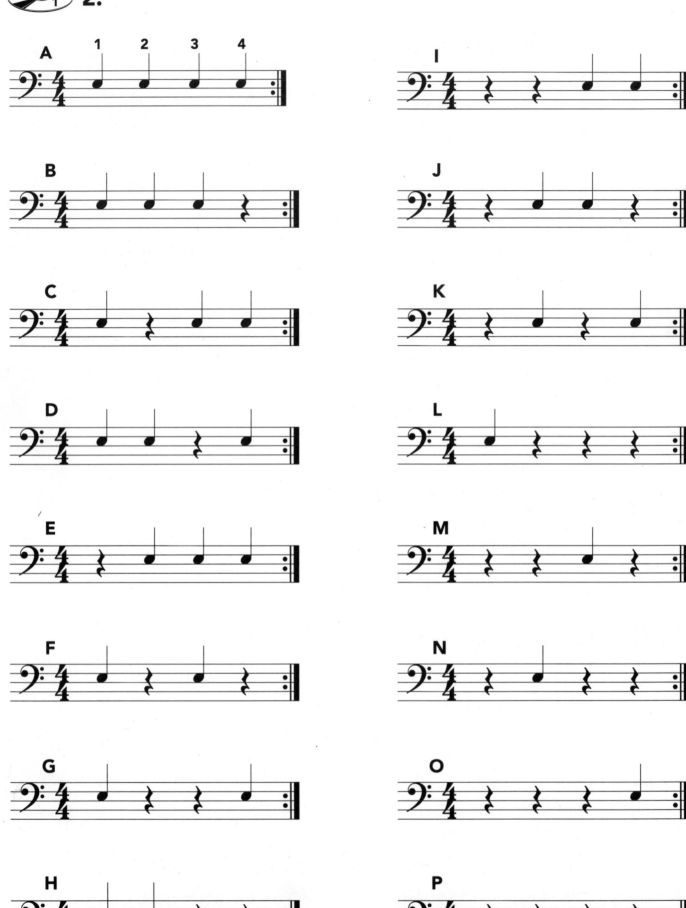

The examples below are 16 bar **sight reading exercises.**
Being able to sight read gives you the following advantages:

1) It quickens the learning process.

2) It gives you a greater understanding of what you play.

3) It allows you to transcribe rhythms and songs and learn them quickly and thoroughly.

4) It broadens your playing prospects by allowing you to play in bands which use charts.

5) It gives you access to vast amounts of written information.

16 bar sight reading exercises featuring the rhythmic figures ♩ and 𝄽·

SIGHT READING EXERCISE 1

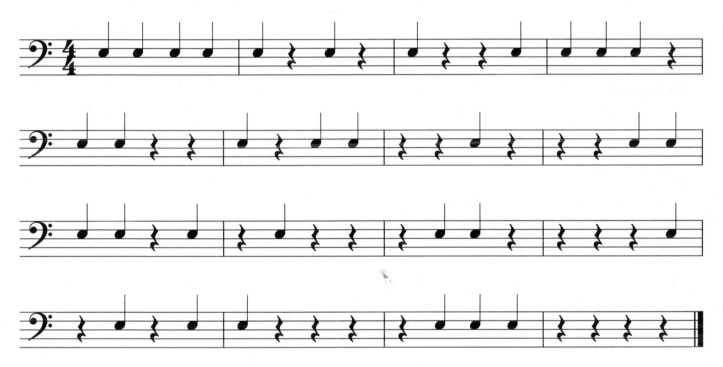

SIGHT READING EXERCISE 2

 **3.0**

In this example the right hand plays a steady quarter note pulse on the hi-hat and the left hand plays the snare drum in unison on beat 3.

 **3.1**

In this example the right hand plays a steady quarter note pulse on hi-hat and the right foot plays the bass drum in unison on beat 1.

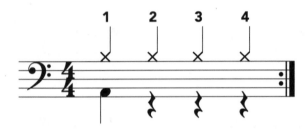

 **3.2**

The bass drum and snare drum alternate in this example.

 3.3

This example combines the previous three and requires three way co-ordination. It is called a **basic rock beat**.

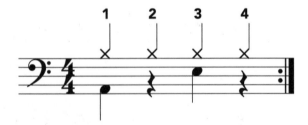

An extra bass drum has been added to beat 3 in the example below.

THE DRUM FILL

A fill is a rhythmical variation from a particular pattern. Any kit part or combination of kit parts may be used. Drum fills are used to 'color' sections of a song and are particularly useful as an indicator of coming changes (e.g. verse to chorus).

 4.0 Below is a simple single stroke fill in bar 2.

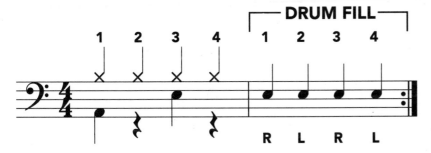

ACCENT

> This symbol indicates that the note is to be played louder.

 4.1 An accented crash cymbal has replaced the hi-hat on beat one of this example

DOUBLE STROKE ROLL

The double stroke roll is another rudiment and consists of two hits per hand.

A double stroke roll is used in the drum fill of this example.

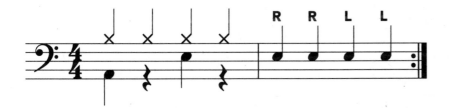

NOTE: Rudiments (also called sticking(s), are sticking exercises which vary the combinations of left and right hand movements.

There are 42 primary rudiments listed in detail on pages 145 to 158. Rudiments facilitate an infinite number of possibilities on drum kit and are the foundation upon which drumming is built.

20

 **5.0**

Below are 3 rhythmic variations for bass drum.

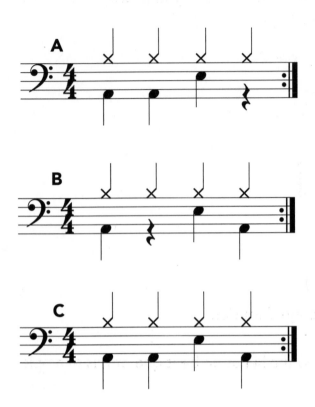

 **5.1**

Here are three rhythmic possibilities for snare drum.

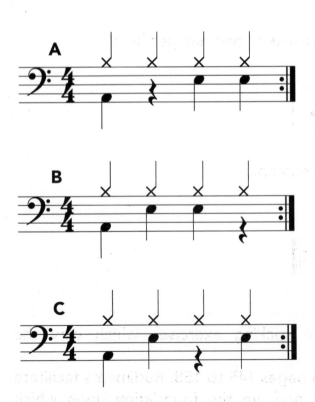

There are a possible **36** two bar rhythms which can be created by joining the 6 one bar patterns on the previous page together in different combinations. The examples below are 6 such possibilities.

THE HALF NOTE

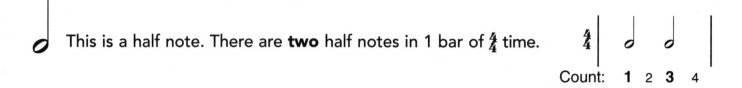

This is a half note. There are **two** half notes in 1 bar of $\frac{4}{4}$ time.

Count: **1** 2 **3** 4

 This is a half note rest and indicates silence for the count of one half note.

SOLO 1

6.

This solo incorporates the patterns covered thus far and introduces the half note rest in the final bar.

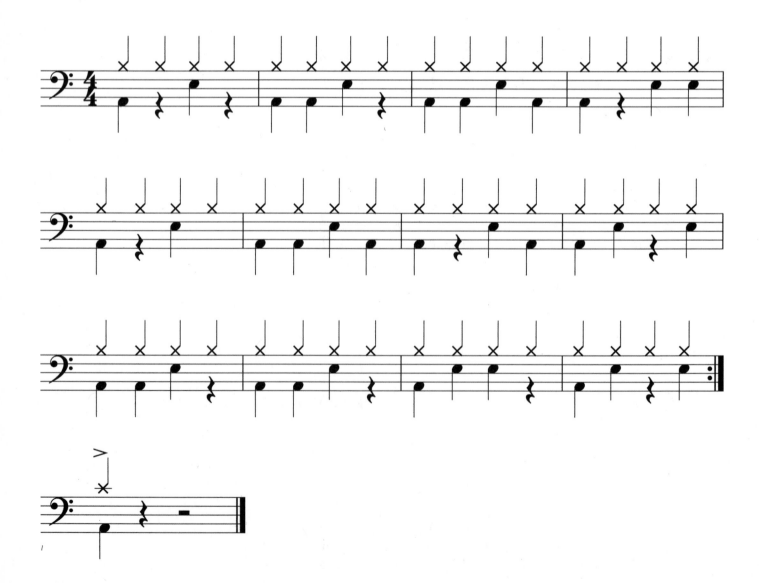

SECTION 2

THE EIGHT NOTE

♪ This is an eighth note and is worth half a count or a half a beat (♩) in ¼ time.
   There are **eight** eighth notes in one bar of ¼ time.
   Groups of two or four eighth notes are joined together with a beam;

e.g.  ← Beam

Beams make reading music easier by helping us distinguish groups of notes.
In ¼ time, eighth notes divide the bar into 8 evenly spaced hits. If the tempo is ♩ = 60,
each bar of ¼ time has a duration of four seconds. Each eighth note hit has a duration of ½ a
second.

Example 7 is played at sixty beats per minute to illustrate the paragraph above.

7.

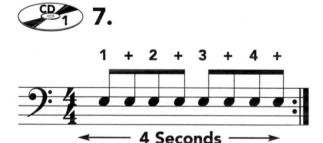

NOTE: Only the digits 1-4 are used when counting in ¼ time. Extra notes are counted
using the following sounds:

   e   pronounced **'ee'**
   +   pronounced **'an'**
   a   pronounced **'uh'**
   r   pronounced **'er'**

At a fixed tempo, eighth notes sound twice as fast as quarter notes because there are
twice as many hits in the same space of time.

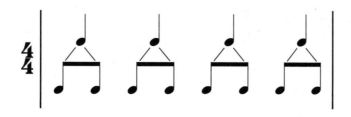

8.

1 bar rhythmic variations featuring the rhythmic figures ♩ and ♫.

16 bar sight reading exercises featuring the rhythmic figures ♩ and ♫.

SIGHT READING EXERCISE 3

SIGHT READING EXERCISE 4

The following 5 examples all contain a fill-in in bar 2. Each fill-in applies previously covered rhythms to different sound sources.

 **9.0**

 **9.1**

 **9.2**

 **9.3**

 **9.4**

THE PARADIDDLE

Below is another rudiment called the **paradiddle**.

If the right hand is moved in a **clockwise** direction around the toms, the example below is created. This right hand movement can be pictured mentally as a triangle (see diagram). thinking in **shapes** benefits memory retention.

10.0

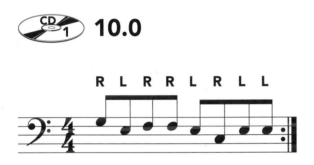

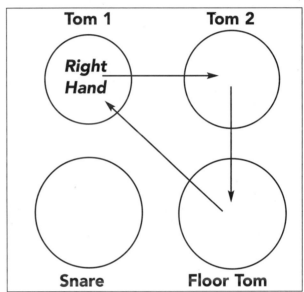

If the right hand starts again on tom 1 but moves in an **anticlockwise** direction, the example below is created.

10.1

This one combines the previous two examples.

SOLO 2

 **11.**

The example below is an 8 bar solo using the paradiddle.

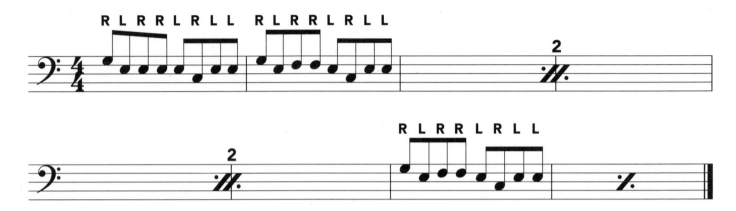

SOLO 3

Here is the same solo with bass drum added to beats 1 and 3 in each bar.

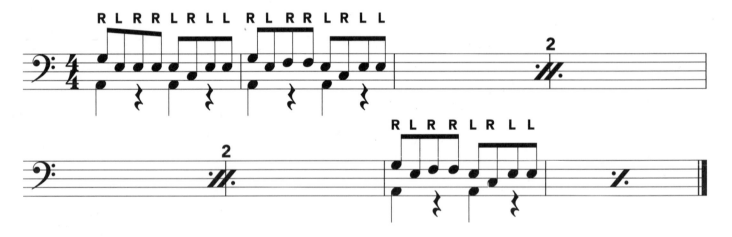

 **12.0**   This paradiddle features two accented notes.

 **12.1**

Bass drum and crash cymbal are played on the accented notes below.

THE EIGHTH NOTE REST

♪ This is an eighth note rest and indicates silence for the count of one eighth note.

SYNCOPATION

Any note or phrase where the rhythmic emphasis (attack) or accent(s) fall on the downbeat(s) (beats 1,2,3 and 4 in 𝄢 time) of a measure is considered non-syncopated.

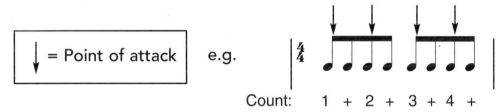

Count: 1 + 2 + 3 + 4 +

Therefore a note or phrase is syncopated when the attack or accent(s) fall on the 'offbeat' (anywhere other than the downbeat).

13. 1 bar rhythmic variations featuring the rhythmic figures ♫ and ♪.

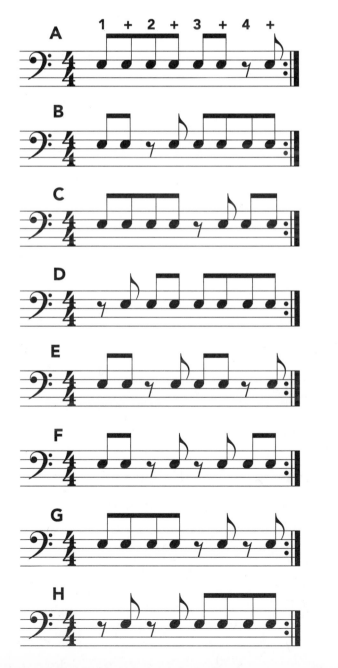

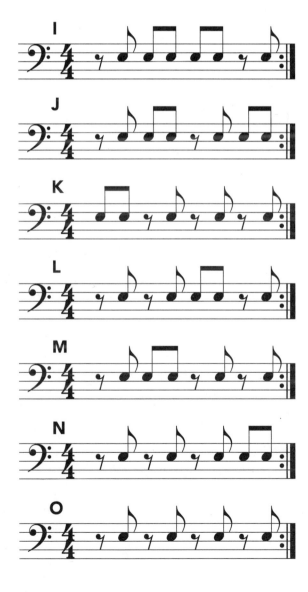

SIGHT READING EXERCISE 5

SIGHT READING EXERCISE 6

 **14.0**

This example features eighth notes on the hi-hat. This is one of the most common hi-hat rhythms in **Rock music.**

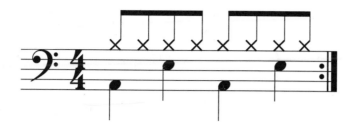

The above pattern should have felt familiar because the combination of notes is exactly the same as example 3.3. The difference is, at a fixed tempo example 14.0 is played twice as fast as example 3.3.

The following four bar pattern illustrates the above.

 **14.1**

$\frac{2}{4}$ TIME

There are 2 x 1/4 notes (or any combination of notes which take up the same space of time as 2 x 1/4 notes) in 1 bar of $\frac{2}{4}$ time. At a fixed tempo, a $\frac{2}{4}$ bar is half the length of a $\frac{4}{4}$ bar.

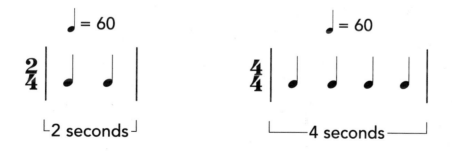

Many of the examples that follow are written in $\frac{2}{4}$ time. Rhythmic possibilities are greatly reduced if written in $\frac{2}{4}$ time rather than $\frac{4}{4}$ time.

e.g. If there are 16 rhythmic variations in $\frac{2}{4}$ time, 256 rhythmic variations in $\frac{4}{4}$ time can be created by joining two bars of $\frac{2}{4}$ together in all possible combinations. Therefore, by practicing 16 rhythmic variations in $\frac{2}{4}$ time the technical facility to create 256 patterns in $\frac{4}{4}$ time has been mastered. This concept can save a great deal of time!

Each of the following 8 examples contain a rhythmic variation for bass drum combined with the following ostinato (repetitive pattern) :

15.

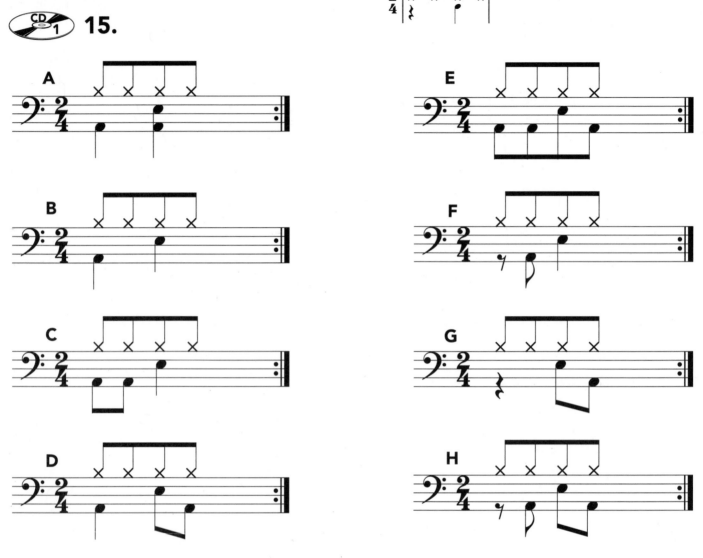

Here are 12 bass drum variations in $\frac{4}{4}$ time. Each is a combination of two of the examples from the previous page. Experiment with your own combinations once these have been mastered.

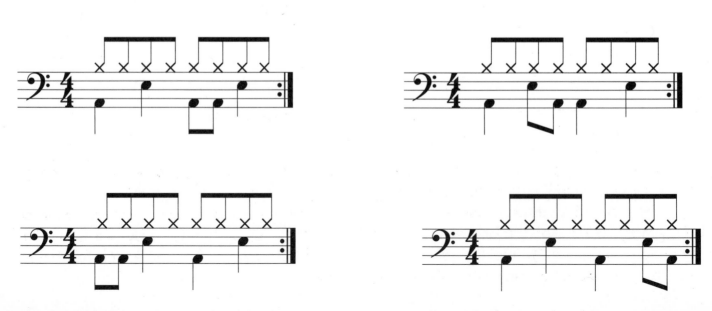

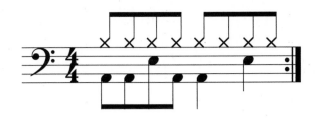

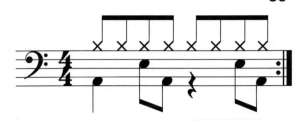

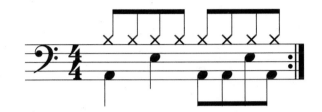

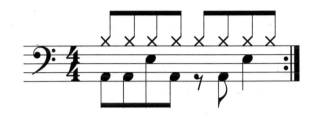

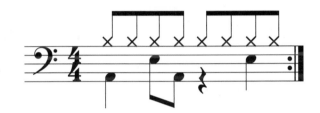

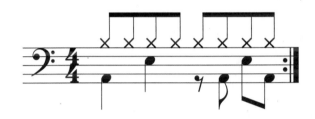

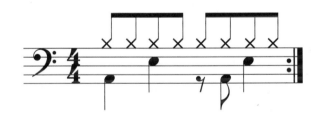

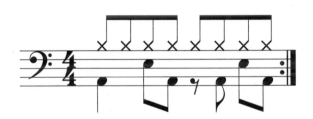

Here are 6 two bar patterns containing rhythmic variations for bass drum. There are 4096 possible variations using the rhythm figures ♩, 𝄽, ♫, and 𝄾♪.

SOLO 4

This solo features rhythmic variations for bass drum using the rhythmic figures ♩, 𝄽, ♫ and ♪.

 **16.**

36

Examples 17A - 17E contain rhythmic variations for snare drum combined with this ostinato:

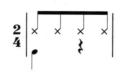

 **17.**

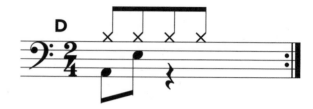

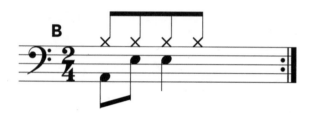

The following 8 examples vary the rhythm of bass drum and snare drum.

 **18.**

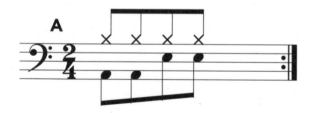

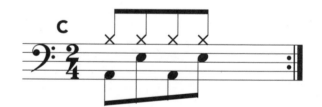

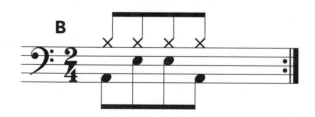

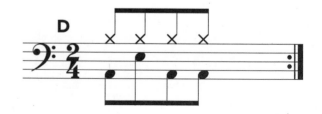

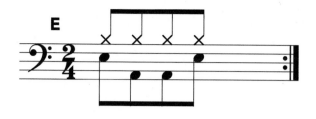

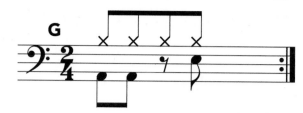

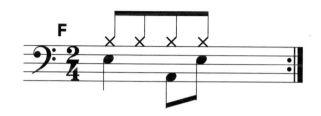

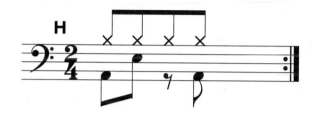

Create your own 4/4 patterns by combining any 2 x 2/4 patterns from the examples on this page, the previous page and page 32.

Here are 6 patterns in 4/4 time containing rhythmic variations for bass drum and snare drum.

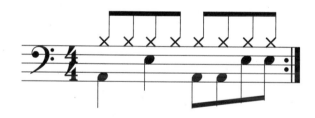

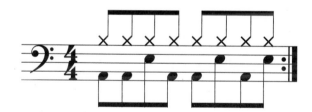

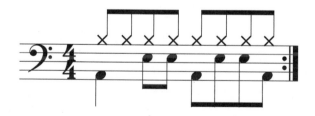

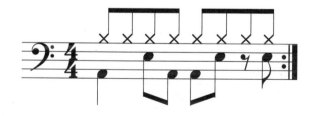

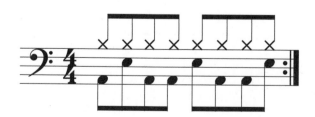

Try these 2 bar patterns:

SOLO 5

This solo features rhythmic variations for snare drum and/or bass drum using the rhythmic figures ♩, 𝄽, ♫ and 𝄾♪.

SECTION 3

THE SIXTEENTH NOTE

 This is a sixteenth note. There are **16** sixteenth notes in 1 bar of ♩ time. Groups of two or four sixteenth notes are joined together with two beams; ♫ or ♬

In ♩ time, sixteenth notes divide the bar into 16 evenly spaced hits. If the tempo is ♩ = 60, each bar of ♩ time has a duration of four seconds. Each sixteenth note hit has a duration of **¼ of a second**.

Example 20 is played at sixty beats per minute to illustrate the paragraph above.

20.

♩ = 60

At a fixed tempo, sixteenth notes sound twice as fast as eighth notes or four times faster than quarter notes.

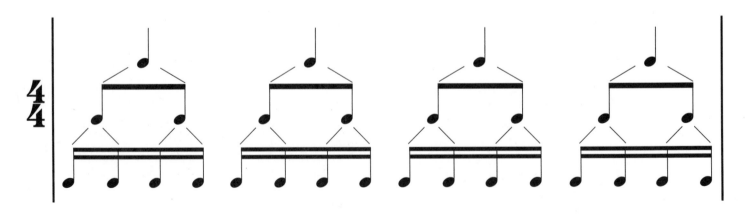

1 bar rhythmic variations featuring the rhythmic figures ♪♪ and ♪♪♪♪.

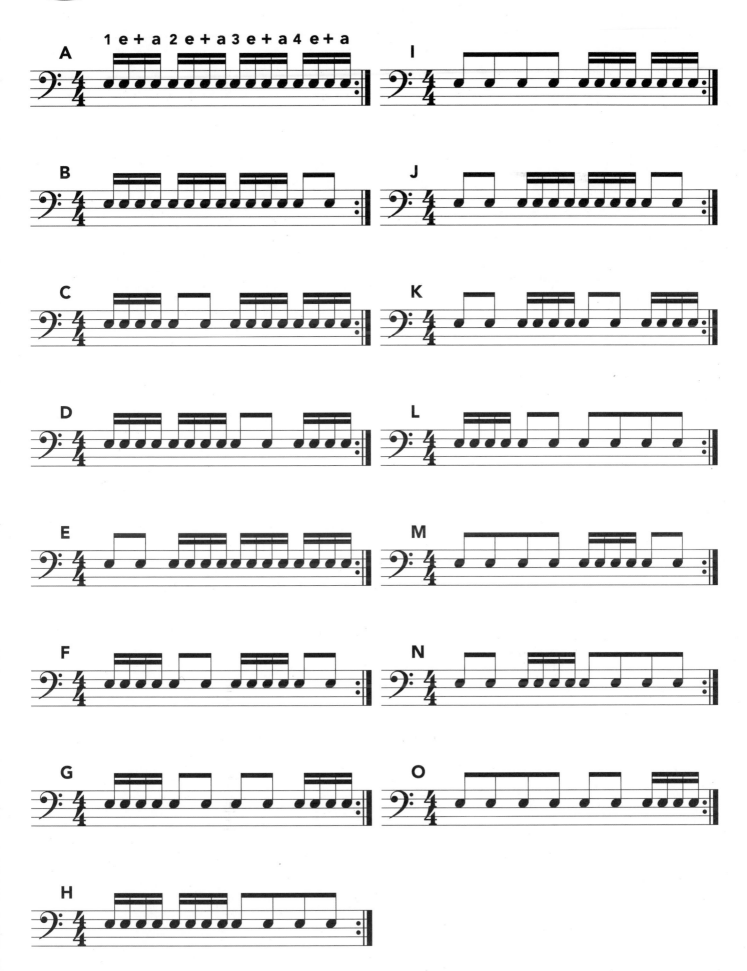

SIGHT READING EXERCISE 7

16 bar sight reading exercise featuring the rhythmic figures ♫ and ♬♬.

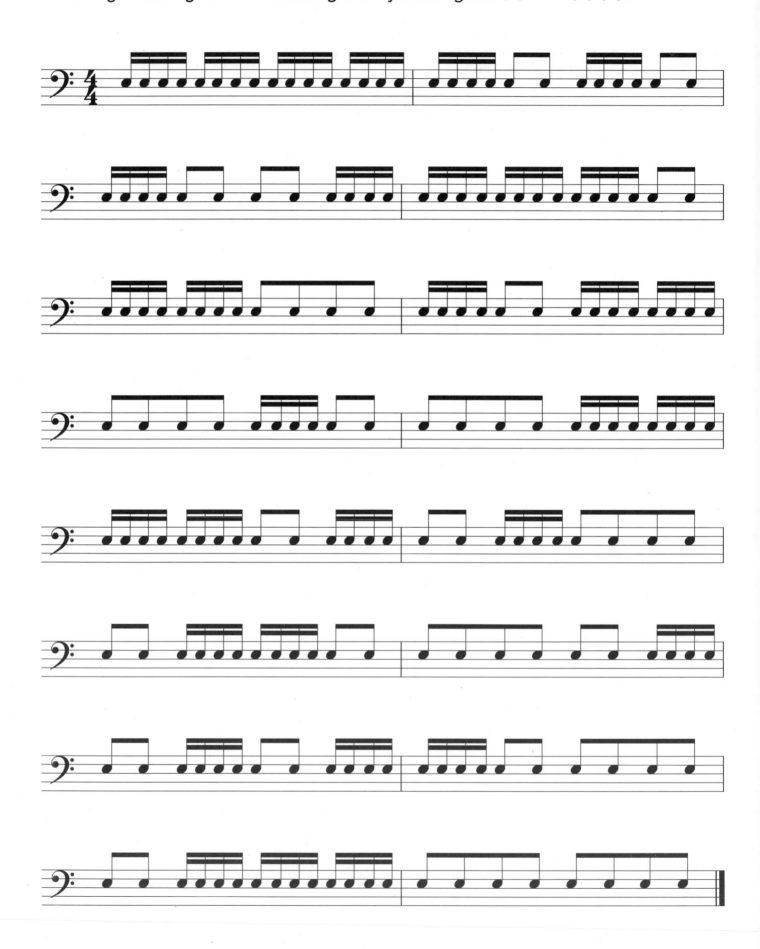

The fill-ins below all feature sixteenth notes.

 **22.0**

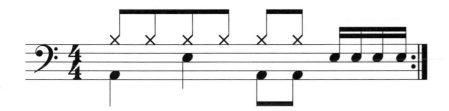

 **22.1**

 **22.2**

 **22.3**

 **22.4**

SIXTEENTH NOTE HI-HAT PATTERNS

Sixteenth notes are used in the hi-hat pattern of the following examples. Each example features rhythmic variations for snare drum and or bass drum using the rhythmic figures ♩, 𝄽, ♫ and 𝄾♪.

CD 1 **23.0**

CD 1 **23.1**

CD 1 **23.2**

CD 1 **23.3**

CD 1 **23.4**

CD 1 **23.5**

SOLO 6

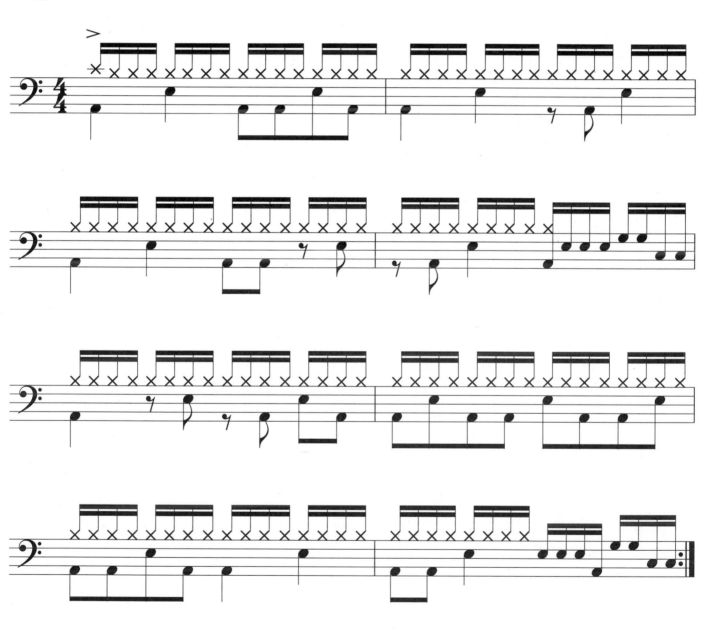

The following examples rely upon the ability to coordinate snare drum or bass drum hits halfway between hi-hat beats.

Examples 25.0 – 25.3 feature commonly used snare drum and or bass drum rhythms.

These 2 bar patterns feature various combinations of examples 25.0 – 25.3 .

SOLO 7

26.

INTRODUCING THE RHYTHMIC FIGURE

1 bar rhythmic variations featuring the rhythmic figures .

27.

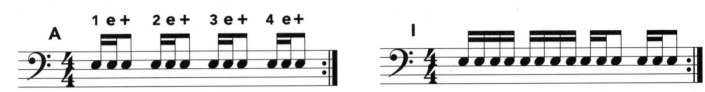

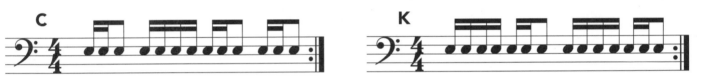

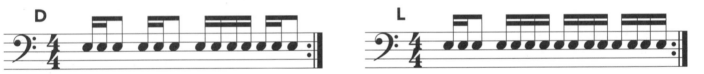

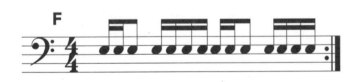

SIGHT READING EXERCISE 8

16 bar sight reading exercise featuring the rhythmic figures ♩♪♪♪♩ and ♪♫♩.

The following fills feature the rhythmic figures ♪♫♫♪ and ♪♫ ♪ 'broken up' between various sound sources.

 **28.0**

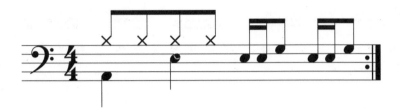

 **28.1**

 **28.2**

OPEN AND CLOSED HI-HATS

The symbol '**o**' indicates that the hi-hat should be struck in a slightly **open** position on that particular beat. The symbol '**x**' indicates the beat in which the hi-hat is **closed.** Experiment with different degrees of openness until you find the sound you like.

 **28.3**

This fill-in features an open hi-hat on beat '4 +'.

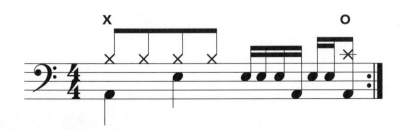

Rhythmic variations incorporating snare drum and or bass drum can be created using the rhythmic figure ♪♪♩. The following examples feature such variations played with a sixteenth note hi-hat pattern.

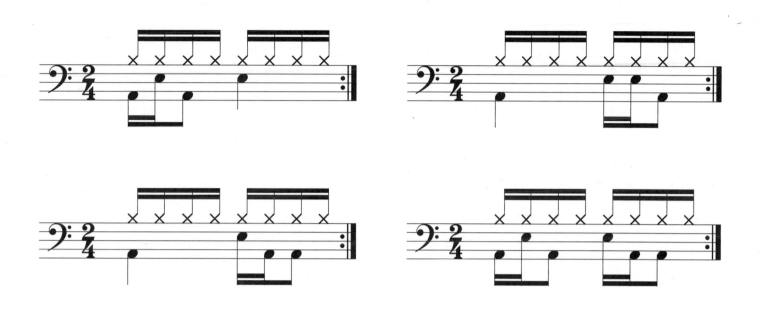

Playing the same rhythmic variations with an eighth note hi-hat pattern requires greater co-ordination. If you're having difficulty with the following examples, try practicing each two part co-ordination possibility first.

     e.g. 1) hi-hat and snare.
        2) hi-hat and kick.
        3) Snare and kick.

CD 1 **29.0**   CD 1 **29.2**

CD 1 **29.1**   CD 1 **29.3**

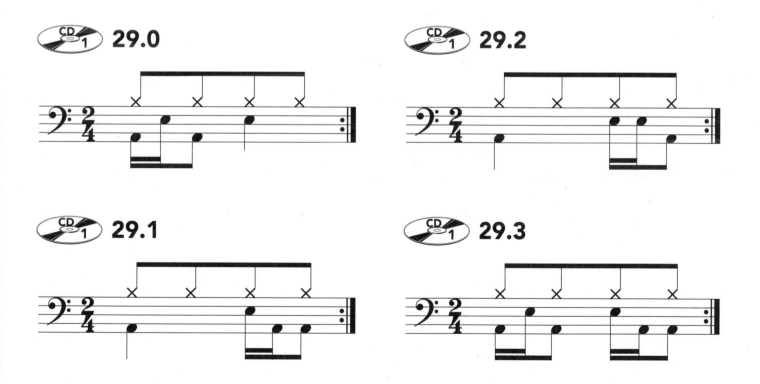

1 bar snare and/or bass drum variations featuring the rhythmic figure ♪♪♩ and previously covered rhythmic figures.

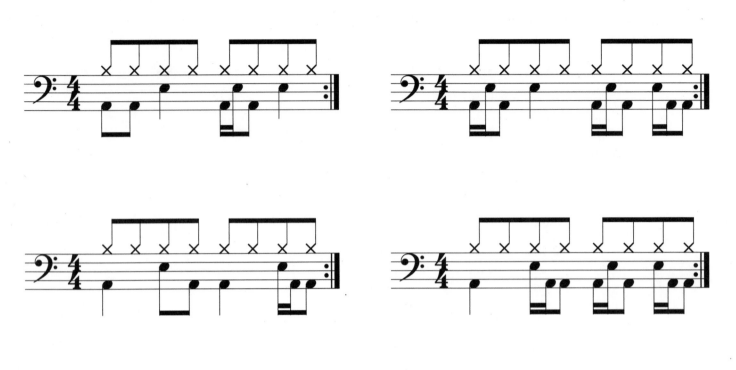

These two bar patterns feature a fill in the second bar.

SOLO 8

This solo features examples from the previous few pages combined with previously covered material.

 **30.**

INTRODUCING THE RHYTHMIC FIGURE

1 bar rhythmic variations featuring the rhythmic figures and .

31.

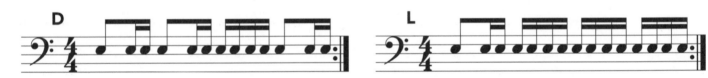

SIGHT READING EXERCISE 9

16 bar sight reading variations featuring the rhythmic figures ♪♫♪ and ♪♫.

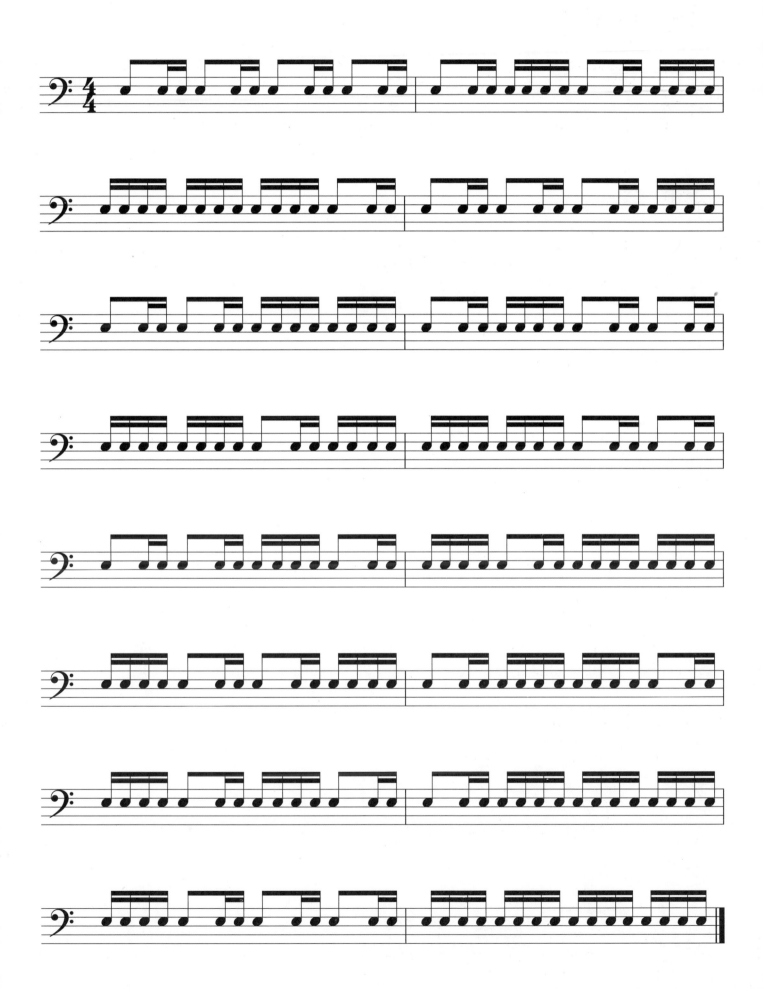

The following fills feature the rhythmic figure ♪ ♫, combined with previously covered rhythmic figures.

 **32.0**

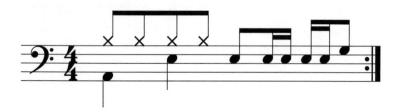

 **32.1**

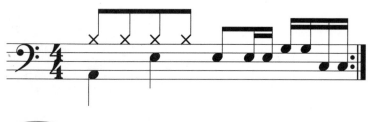

 **32.2**

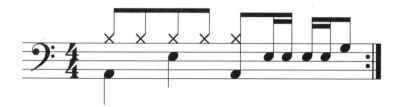

THE FLAM

A flam consists of a grace note (♪) which is tied to a principle note (♪). The grace note is played at a lesser volume, fractionally before the principle note. Only the principle note has a specific note value. Examples 32.3 and 32.4 feature a flam on beat '4'.

Rhythmic variations incorporating snare drum and or bass drum can be created using the rhythmic figure ♩ ♫ . The following examples feature such variations played with a sixteenth note hi-hat pattern.

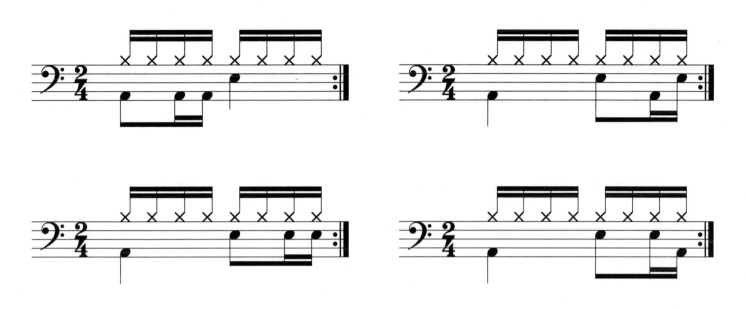

Here are the same rhythmic variations with an eighth note hi-hat pattern.

33.0

33.2

33.1

33.3

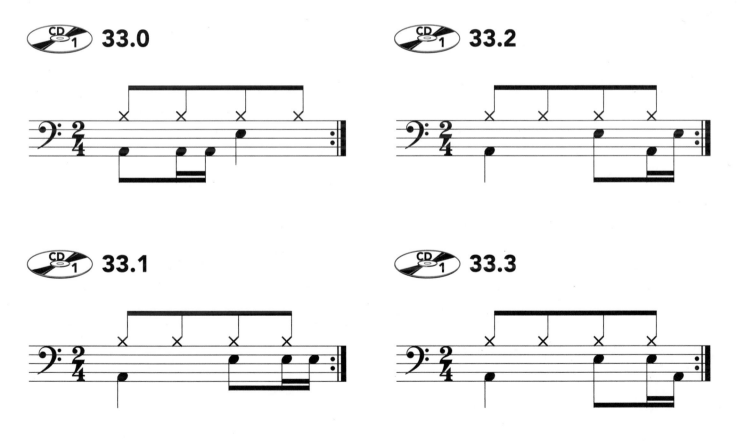

1 bar snare and/or bass drum variations featuring the rhythmic figure ♪♫ and previously covered rhythmic figures.

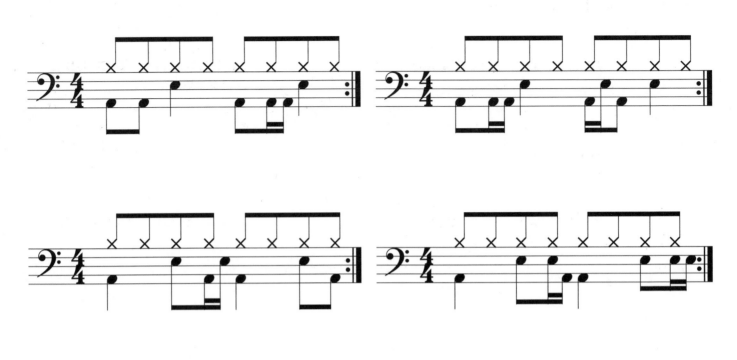

2 bar patterns featuring a fill over the last 2 beats.

SOLO 9

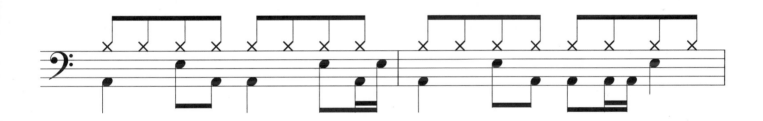

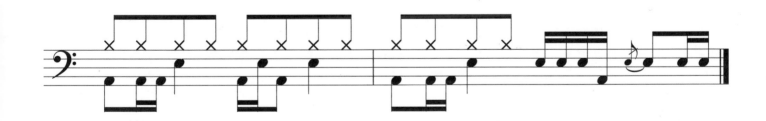

THE DOT

A dot after a note increases its value by half e.g.   Dotted Quarter Note: ♩. = ♩ + ♪

Dotted Half Note: ♪. = ♪ + ♪

Only play first note

INTRODUCING THE RHYTHMIC FIGURE

1 bar rhythmic variations featuring the rhythmic figures ♫♫ and ♩. ♪.

35.

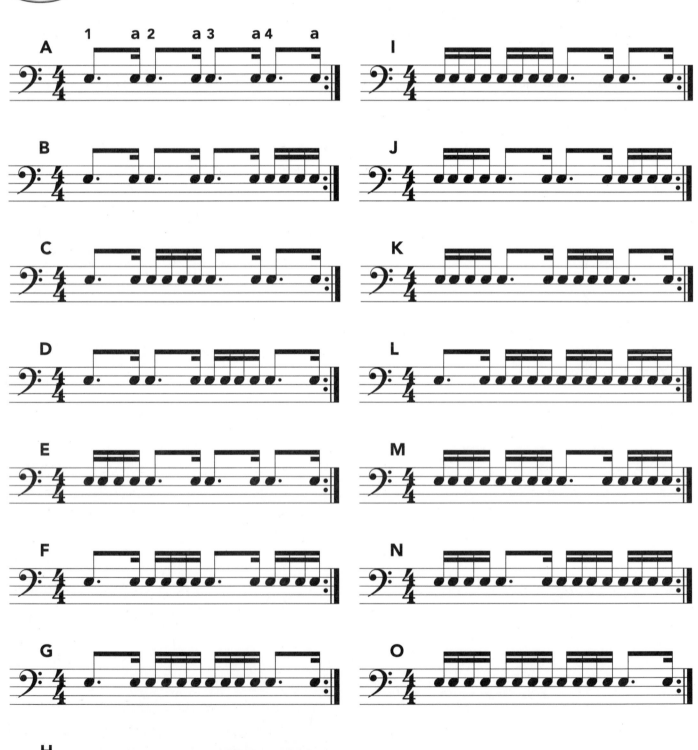

SIGHT READING EXERCISE 10

16 bar sight reading exercise featuring the rhythmic figures ♪♪♪♪ and ♩. ♪.

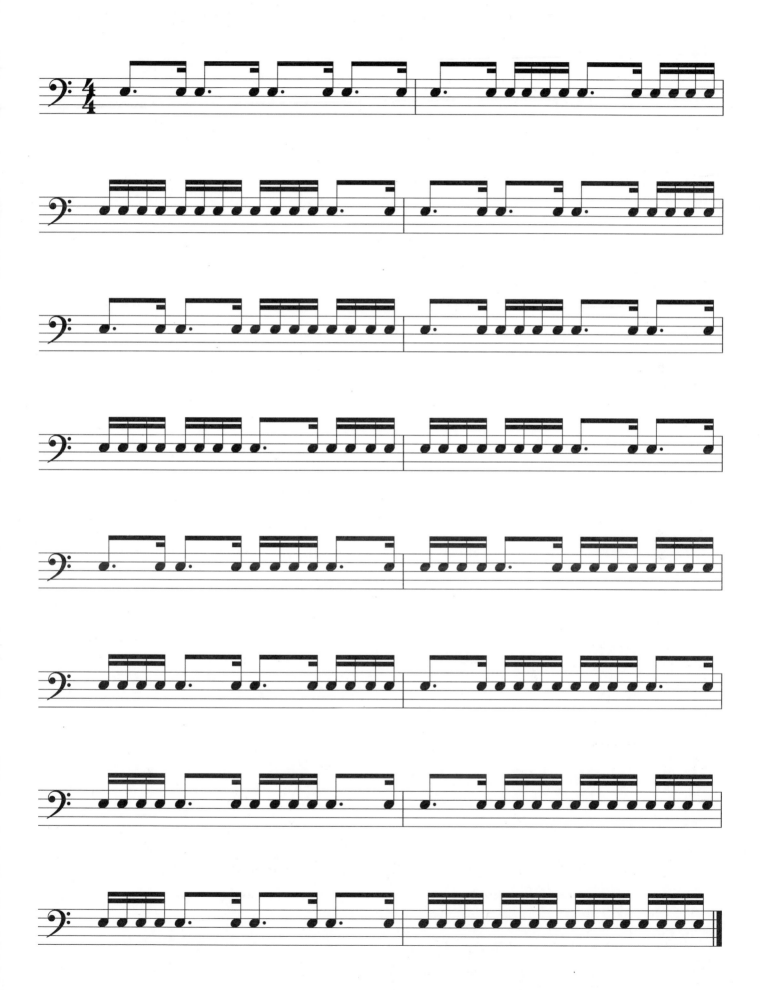

Rhythmic variations for snare drum and or bass drum featuring the rhythmic figure

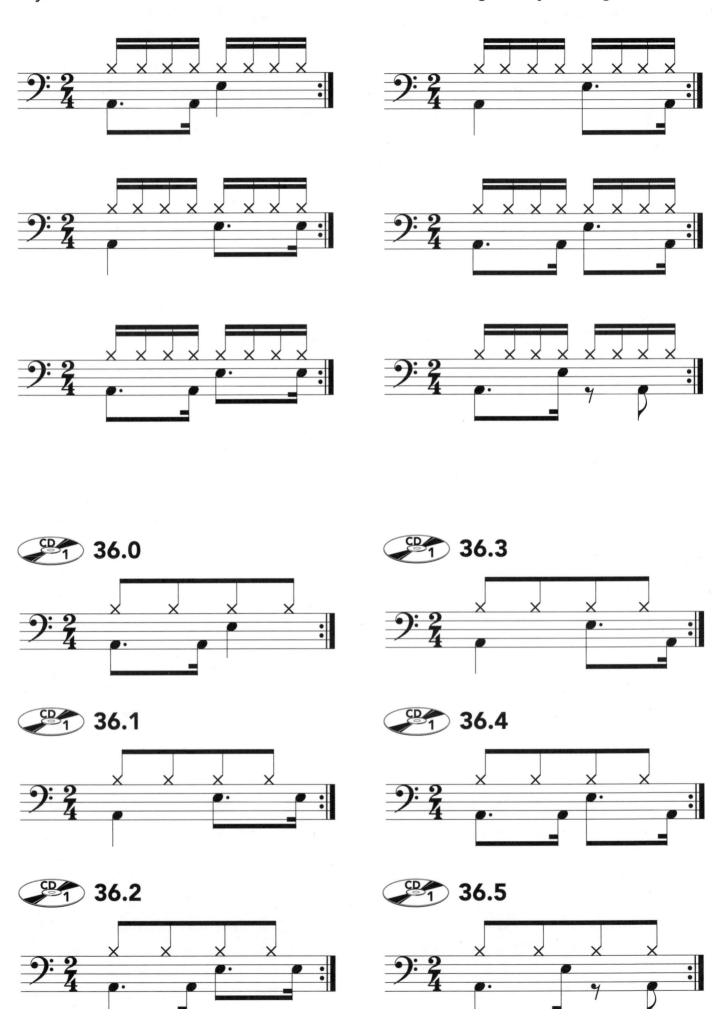

1 bar snare and/or bass drum variations featuring the rhythmic figure ♩. ♪ and previously covered rhythmic figures.

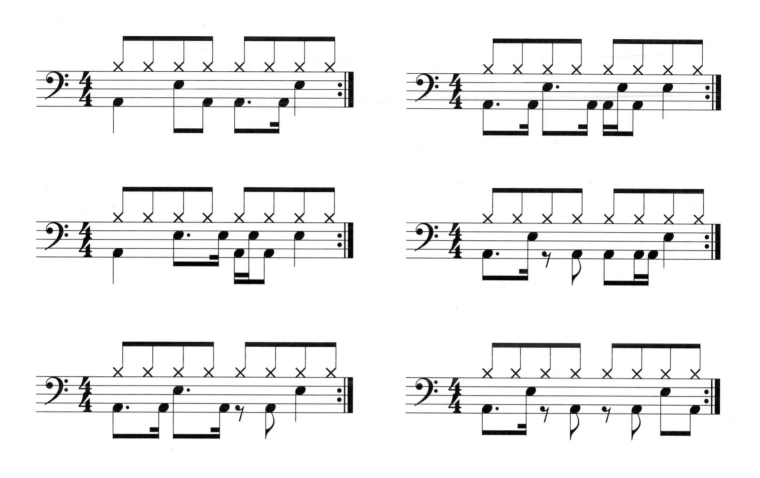

2 bar patterns featuring a fill over the last 2 beats.

SOLO 10

 **37.**

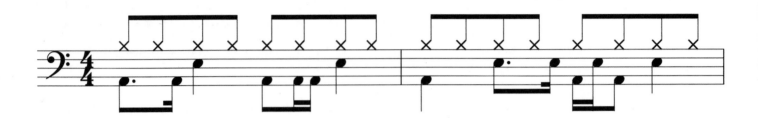

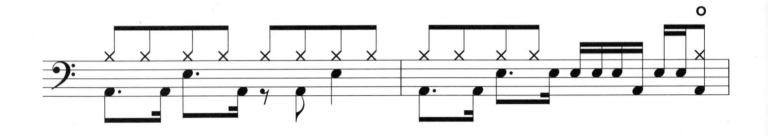

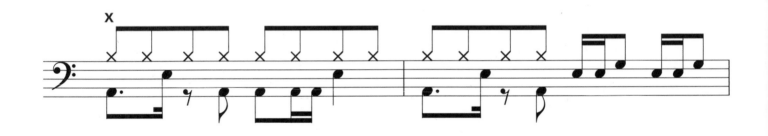

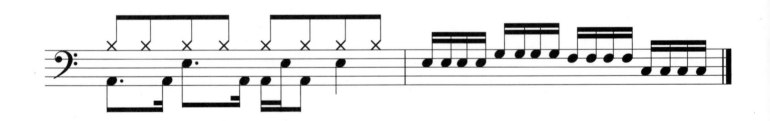

INTRODUCING THE RHYTHMIC FIGURE

1 bar rhythmic variations featuring the rhythmic figures ♫♫ and ♪♫.

38.

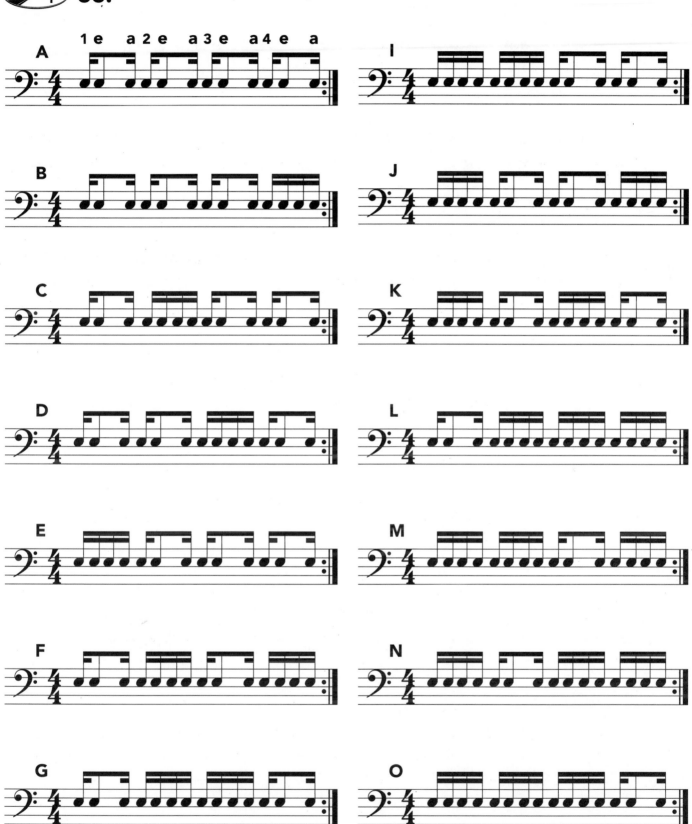

SIGHT READING EXERCISE 11

16 bar sight reading exercise featuring the rhythmic figures and .

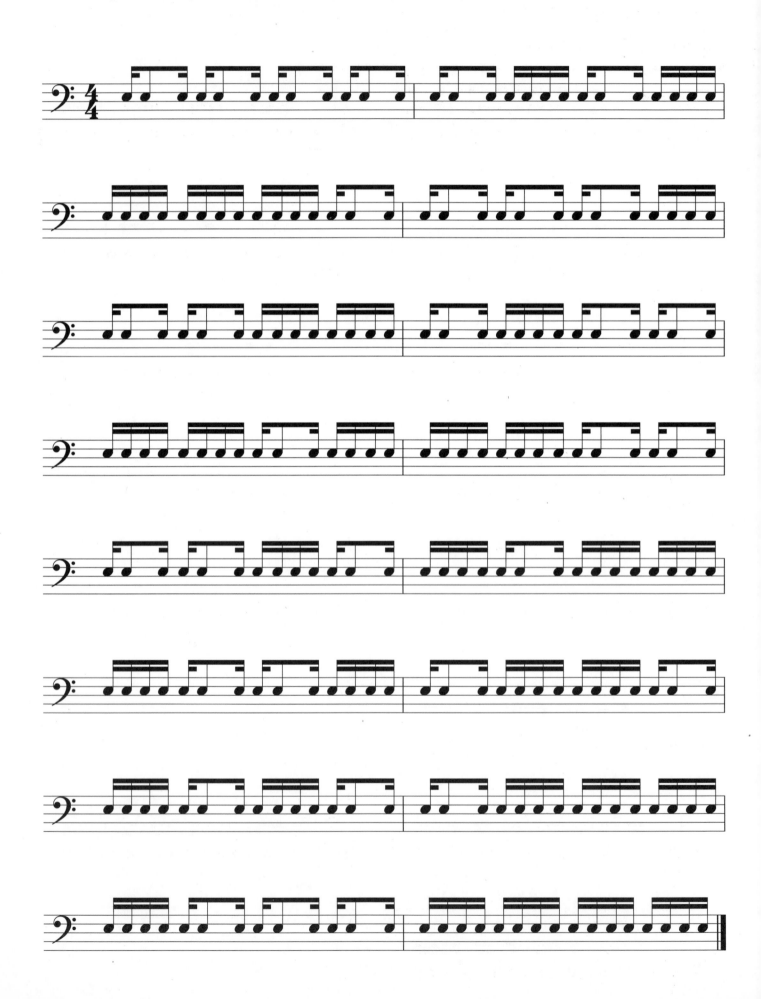

The following fills feature the rhythmic figure , combined with previously covered rhythmic figures.

39.0

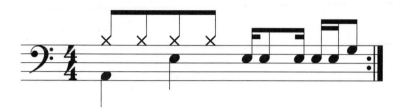

39.1

39.2

39.3

39.4

39.5

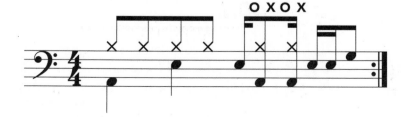

Rhythmic variations for snare drum and or bass drum featuring the rhythmic figure ♪♪♫.

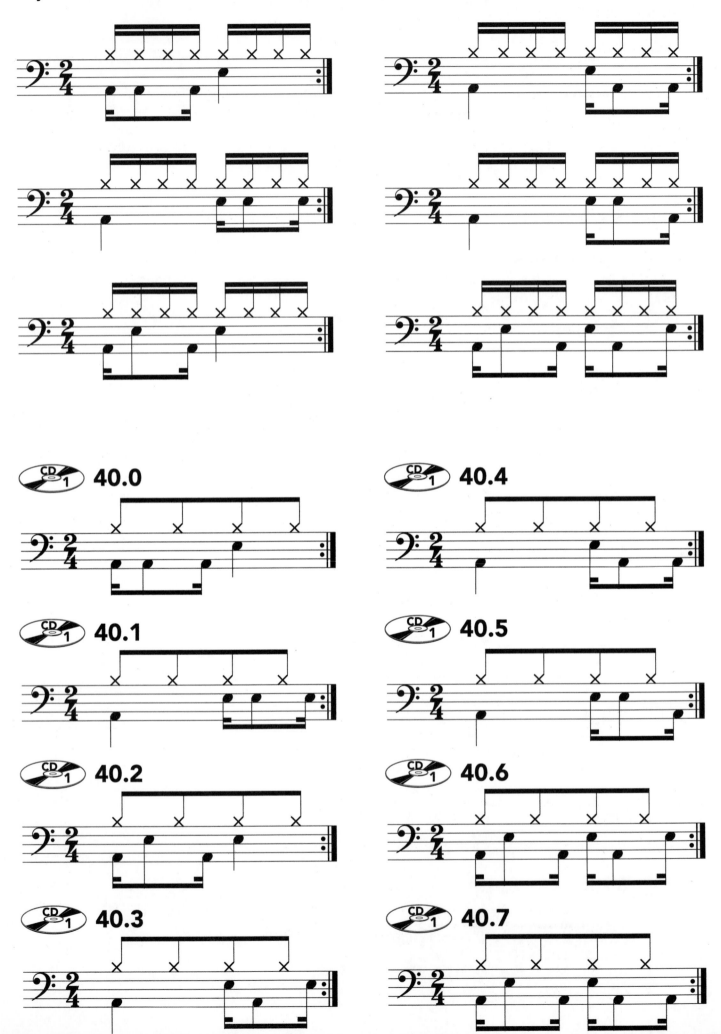

1 bar snare and/or bass drum variations featuring the rhythmic figure ♪♪♩ and previously covered rhythmic figures.

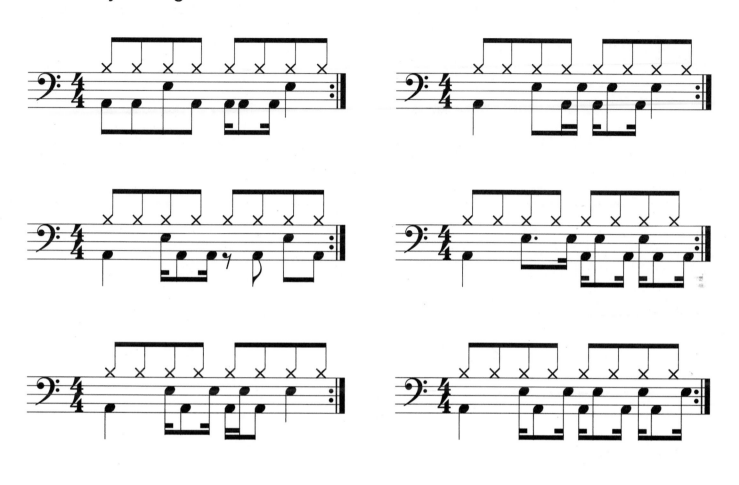

2 bar patterns featuring a fill over the last two beats.

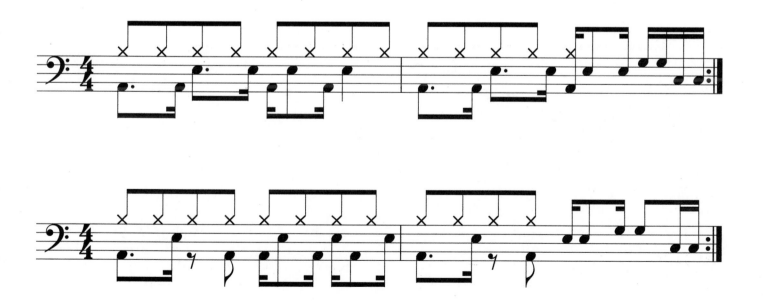

SOLO 11

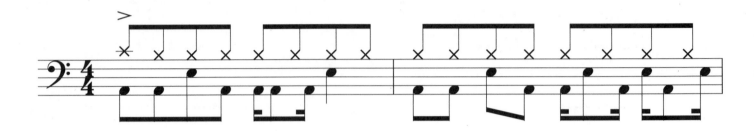

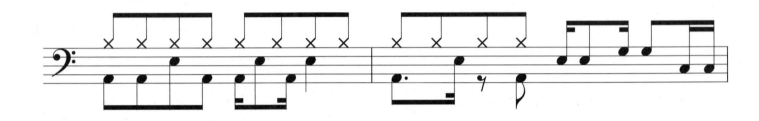

THE SIXTEENTH NOTE REST

 This is a sixteenth note rest and indicates silence for the count of one sixteenth note.

INTRODUCING THE RHYTHMIC FIGURE

1 bar rhythmic variations featuring the rhythmic figures and .

42.

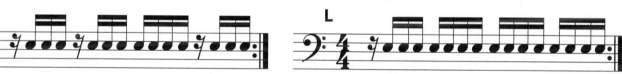

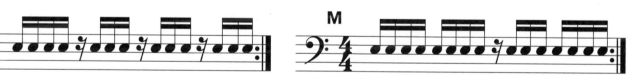

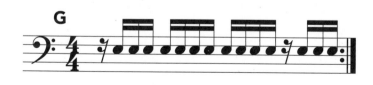
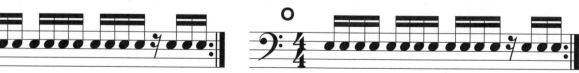

SIGHT READING EXERCISE 12

16 bar sight reading exercise featuring the rhythmic figures 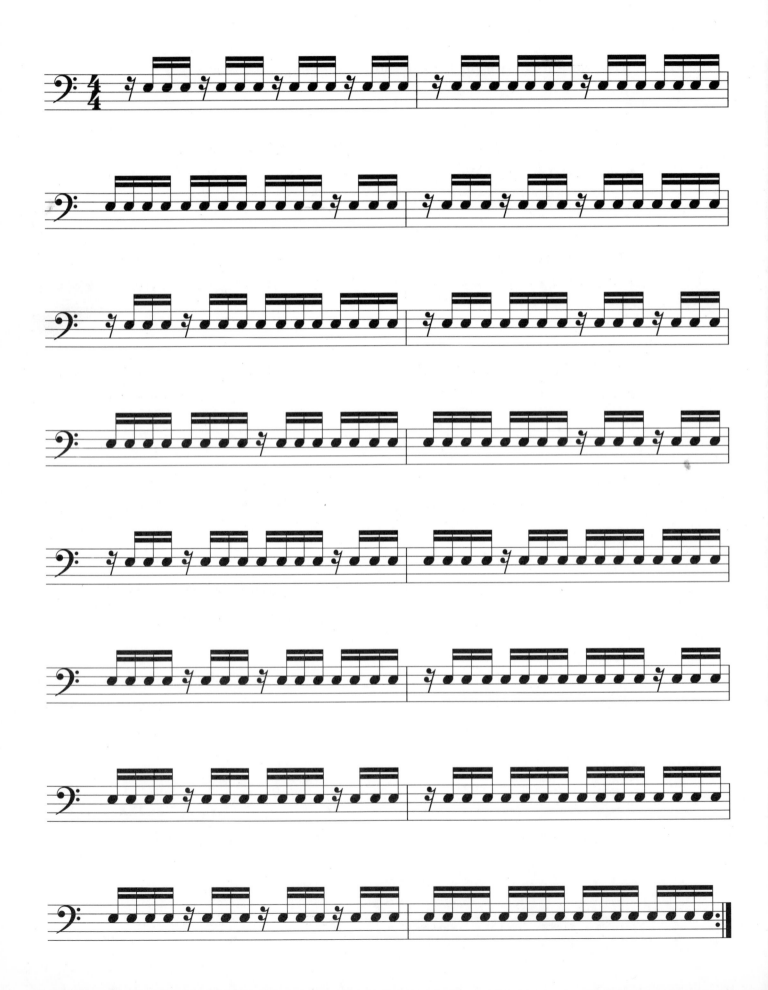 and ♪.

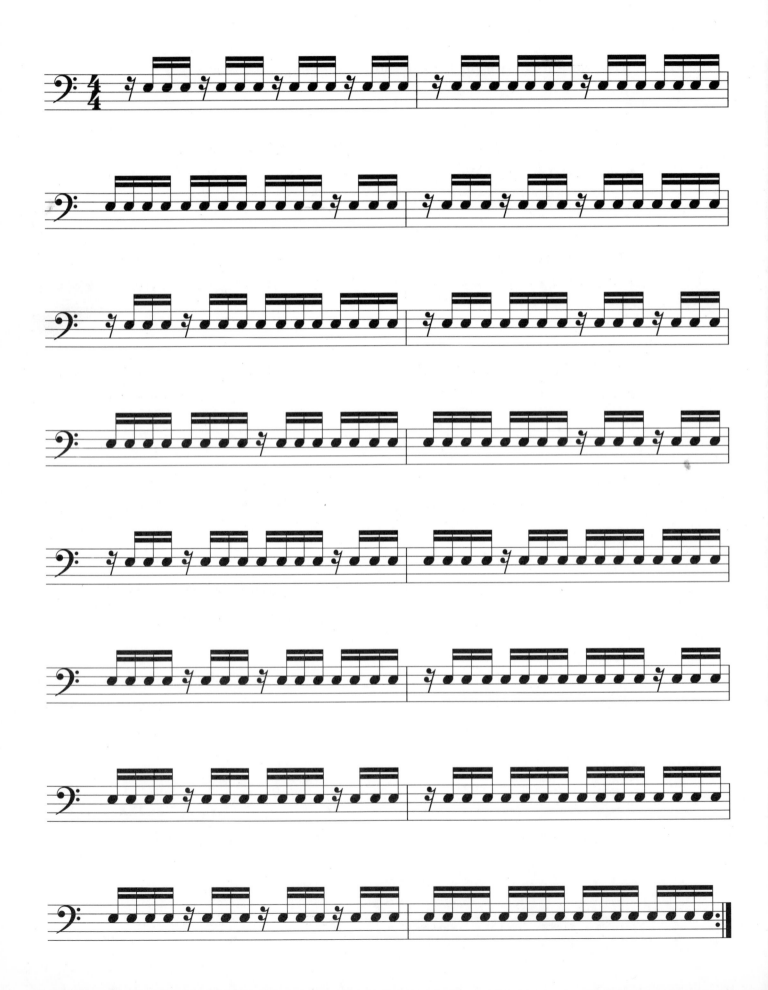

The following fills feature the rhythmic figure , combined with previously covered rhythmic figures.

 **43.0**

 **43.1**

 **43.2**

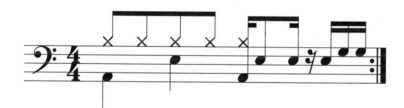

 **43.3**

 **43.4**

Rhythmic variations for snare and bass drum featuring the rhythmic figure ♪ ♫ ♪.

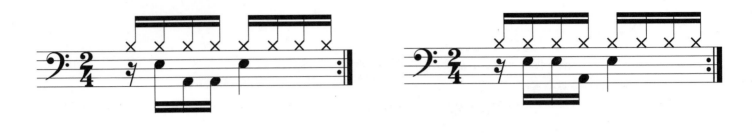

CD 1 **44.0**   CD 1 **44.1**

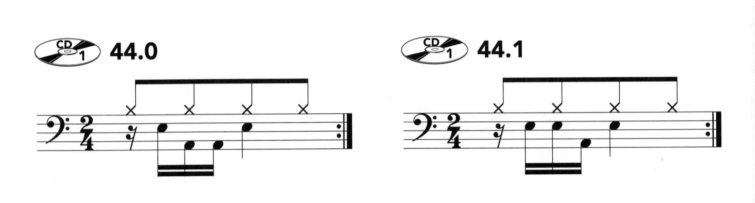

1 bar snare and bass drum variations featuring the rhythmic figure ♪ ♫ ♪ and previously covered rhythmic figures.

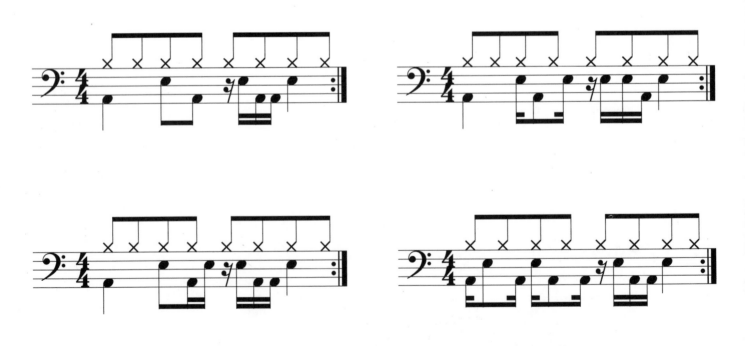

SOLO 12

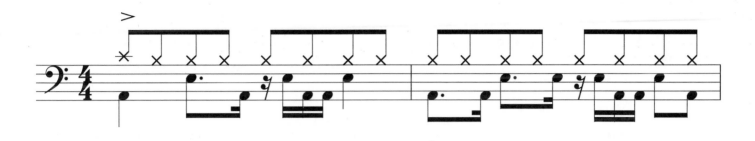

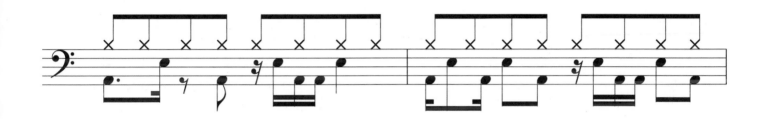

INTRODUCING THE RHYTHMIC FIGURE

1 bar rhythmic variations featuring the rhythmic figures and .

46.

SIGHT READING EXERCISE 13

16 bar sight reading exercise featuring the rhythmic figures ♪♫♫♪ and ♪♫.

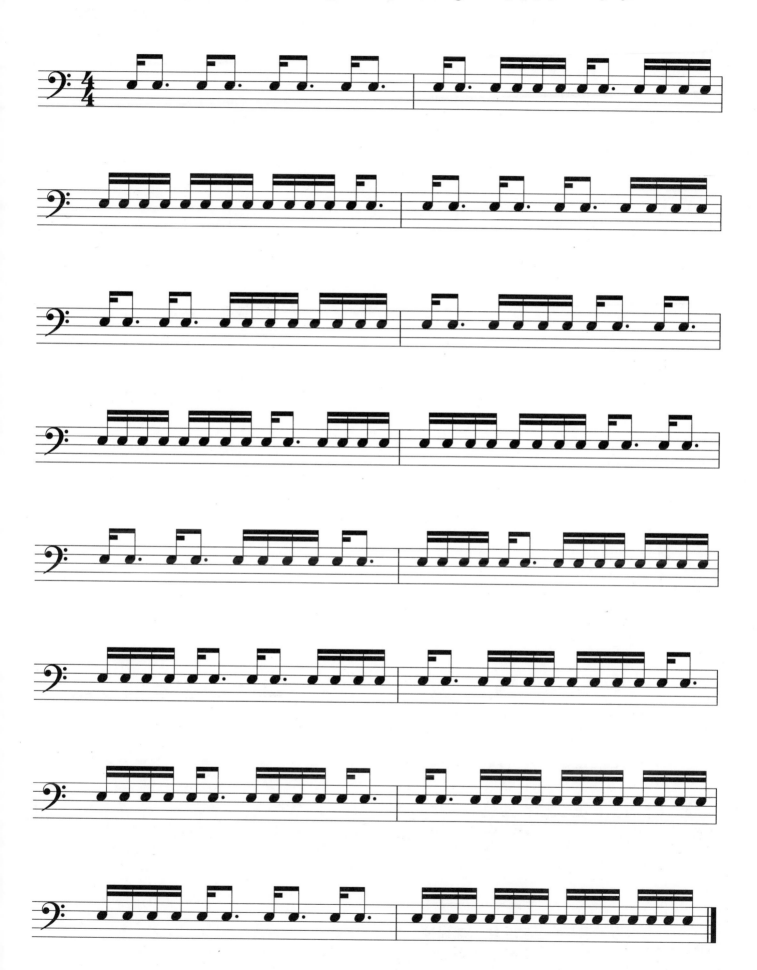

Rhythmic variations for bass drum, featuring the rhythmic figure ♫.

CD 1 **47.0**

CD 1 **47.2**

CD 1 **47.1**

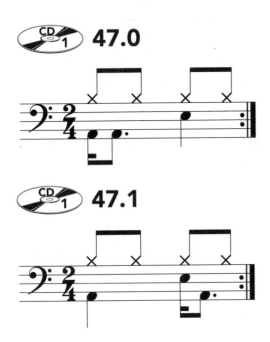

1 bar snare and/or bass drum variations featuring the rhythmic figure ♫. and previously covered rhythmic variations.

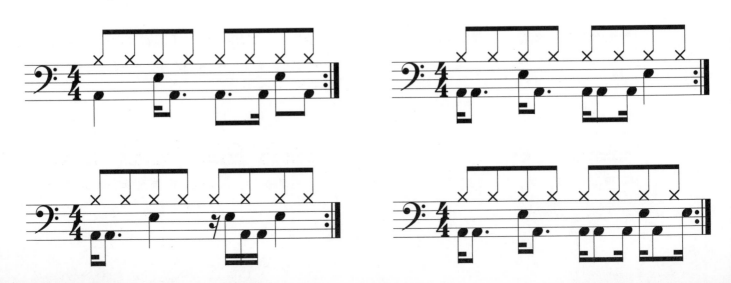

SOLO 13

 48.

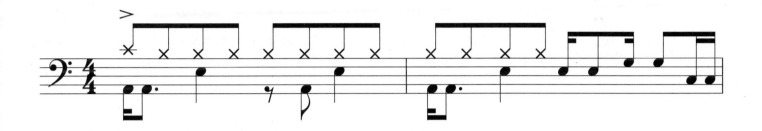

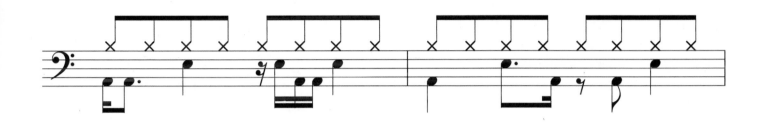

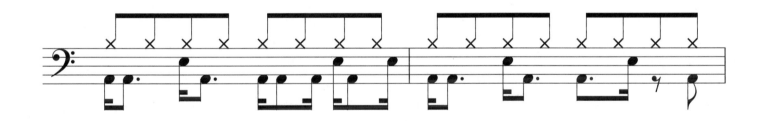

INTRODUCING THE RHYTHMIC FIGURE

1 bar rhythmic variations featuring the rhythmic figures  and .

🔘 49.

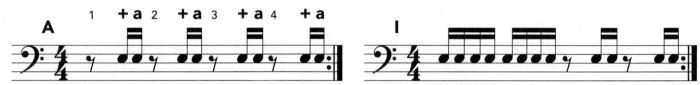

SIGHT READING EXERCISE 14

16 bar sight reading exercise featuring the rhythmic figures ♩♫♩ and ⅄♫.

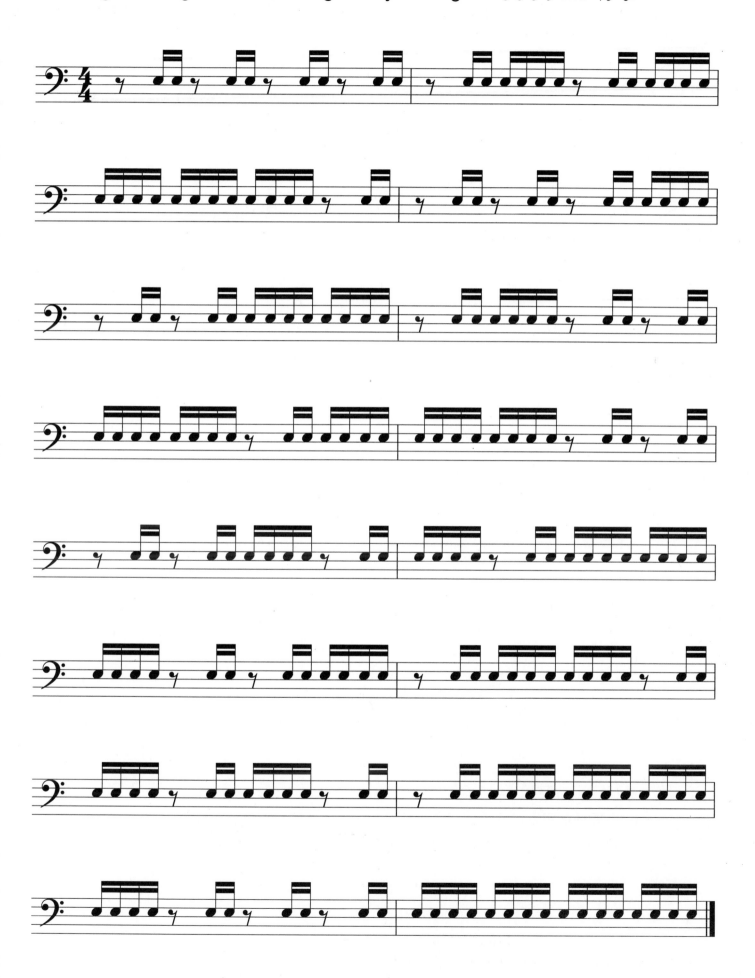

Rhythmic variations for bass drum featuring the rhythmic figure

CD 1 **50.1**

CD 1 **50.2**

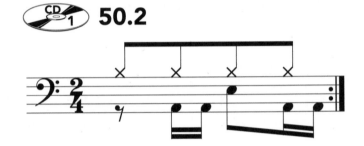

1 bar variations.

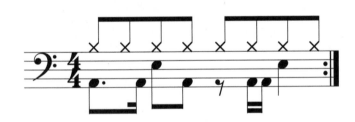

SOLO 14

 **51.**

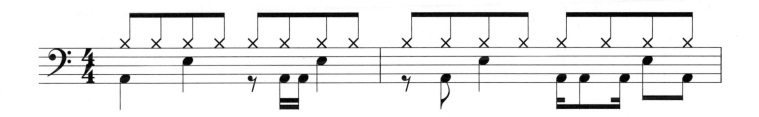

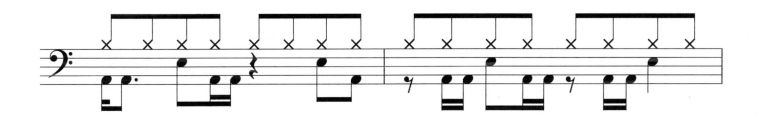

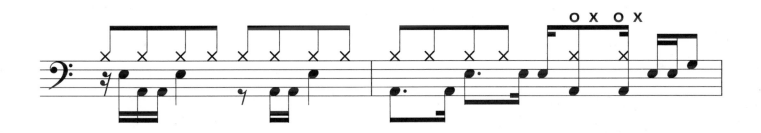

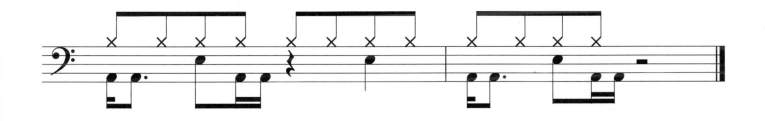

INTRODUCING THE RHYTHMIC FIGURE

1 bar rhythmic variations featuring the rhythmic figures and .

CD 1 **52.**

A

I

B

J

C

K

D

L

E

M

F

N

G

O

H

SIGHT READING EXERCISE 15

16 bar sight reading exercise featuring the rhythmic figures 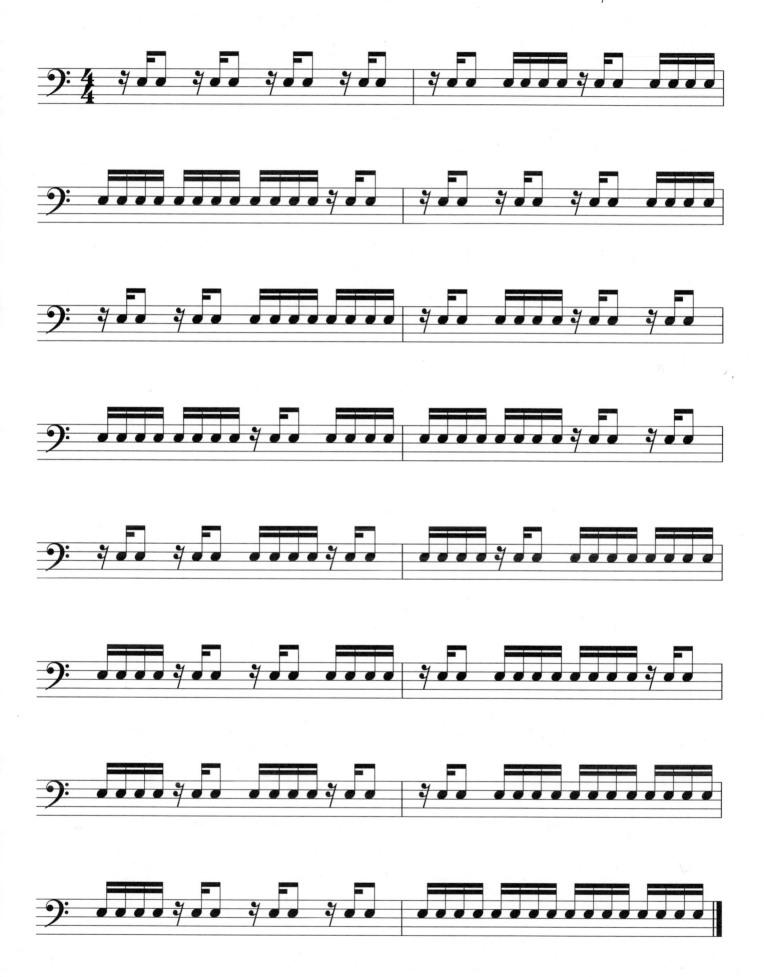 and .

Rhythmic variations for snare and or bass drum featuring the rhythmic figure.

CD 1 **53.0**

CD 1 **53.1**

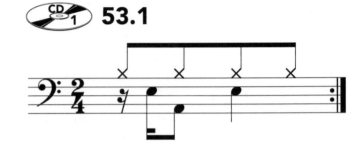

1 bar variations.

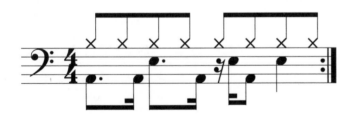

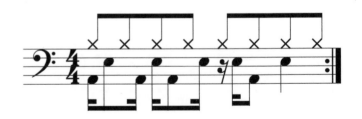

SOLO 15

54.

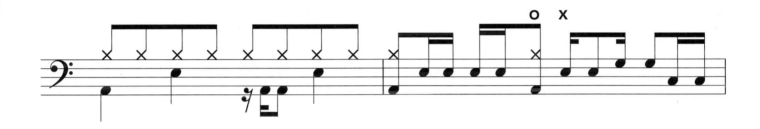

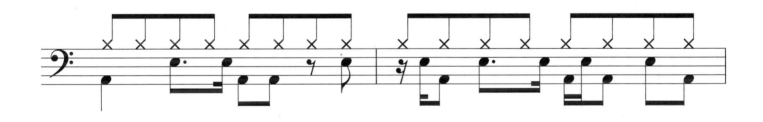

INTRODUCING THE RHYTHMIC FIGURE

1 bar rhythmic variations featuring the rhythmic figures  and .

55.

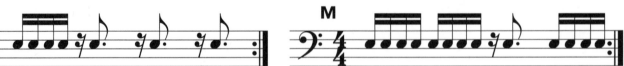

SIGHT READING EXERCISE 16

16 bar sight reading exercise featuring the rhythmic figures and .

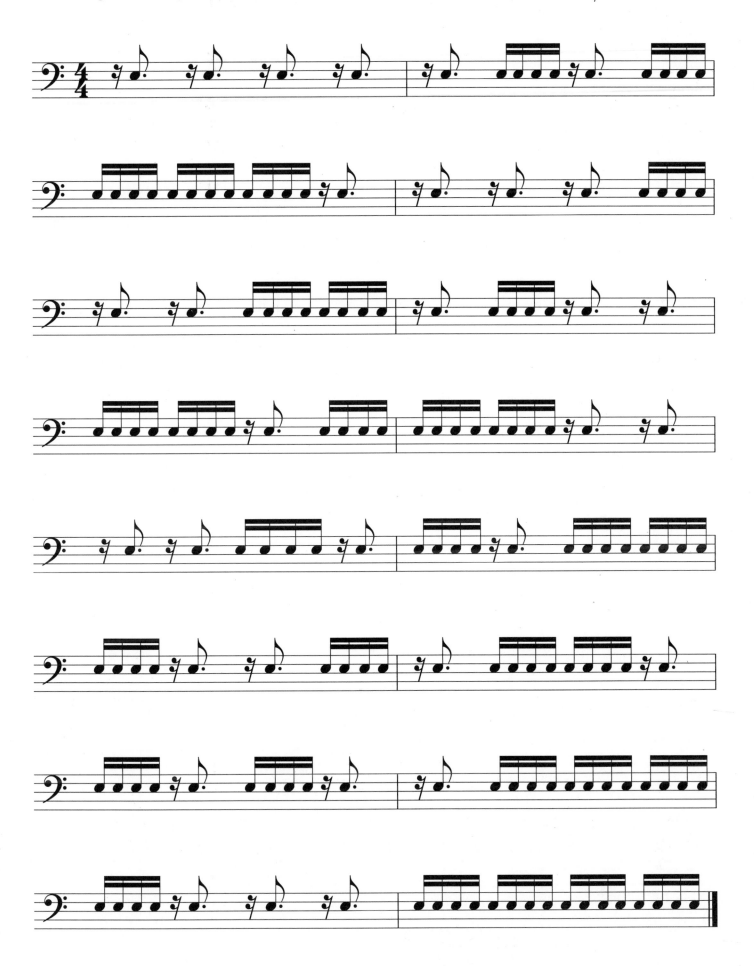

INTRODUCING THE RHYTHMIC FIGURE

1 bar rhythmic variations featuring the rhythmic figures and .

SIGHT READING EXERCISE 17

16 bar sight reading exercise featuring the rhythmic figures ♪♫♫♪ and ♪. ♪.

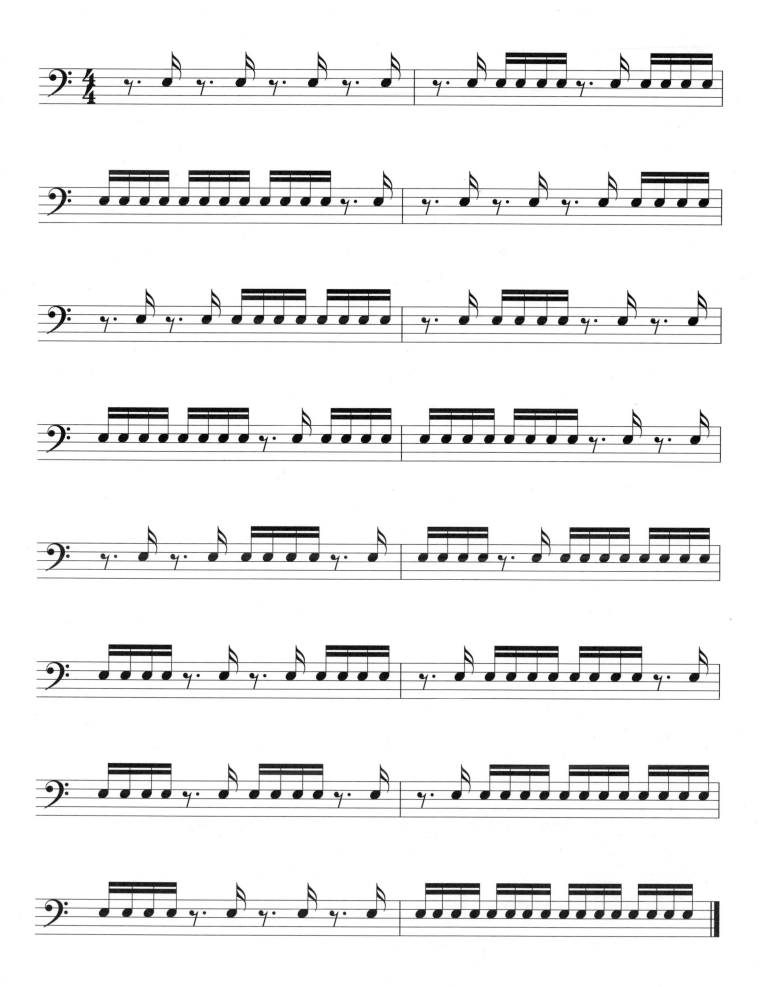

INTRODUCING THE RHYTHMIC FIGURE

1 bar rhythmic variations featuring the rhythmic figures and .

57.

SIGHT READING EXERCISE 18

16 bar sight reading exercise featuring the rhythmic figures and .

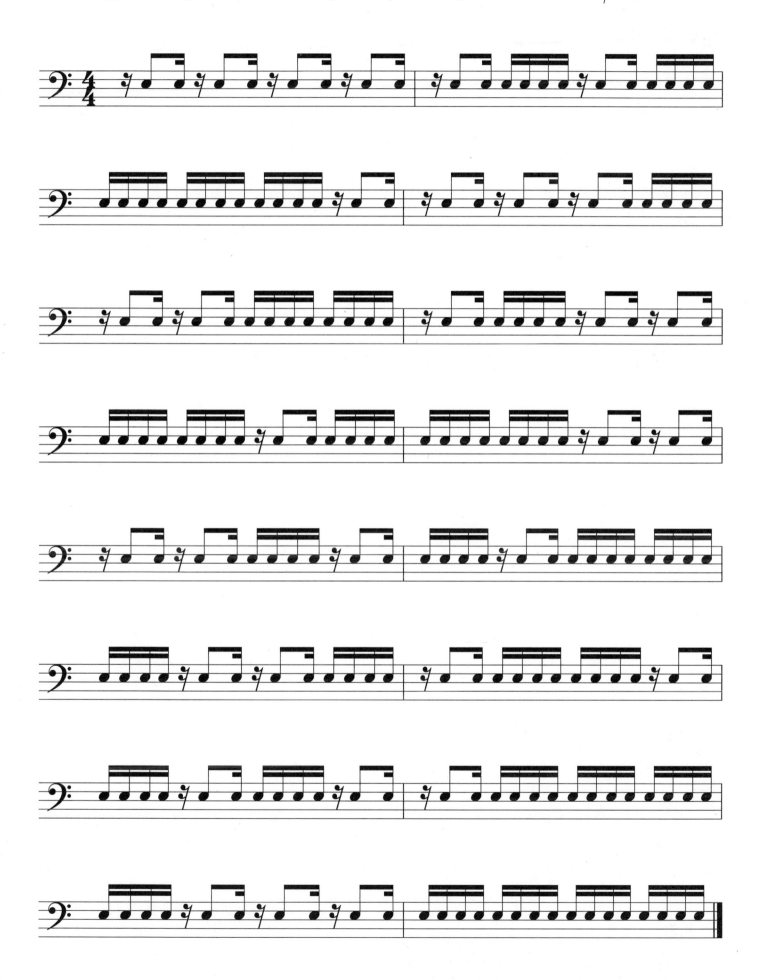

Rhythmic variations for snare and or bass drum featuring the rhythmic figures ♪♩. , ♩.♪ and ♩♫.

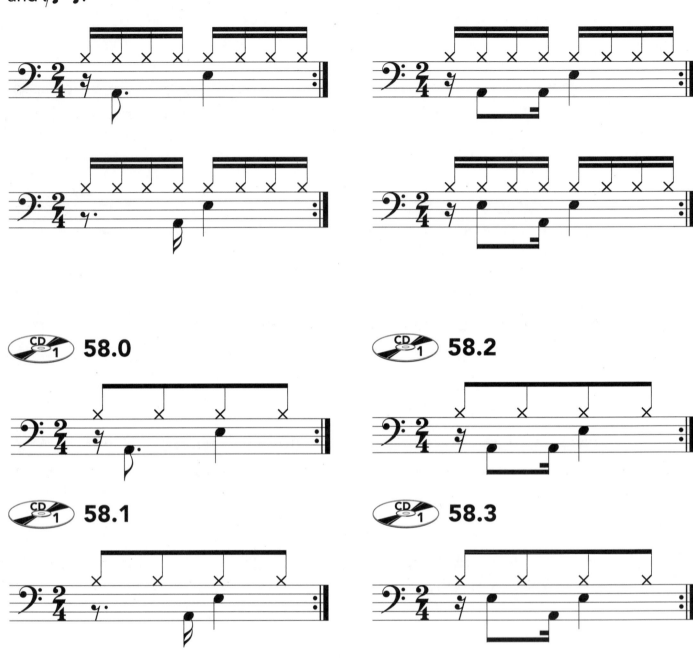

CD1 **58.0**

CD1 **58.1**

CD1 **58.2**

CD1 **58.3**

1 bar variations.

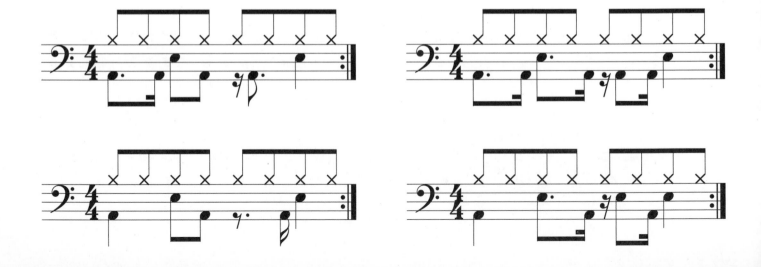

SOLO 16

59.

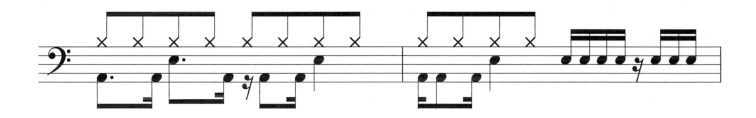

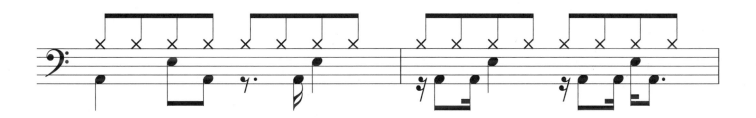

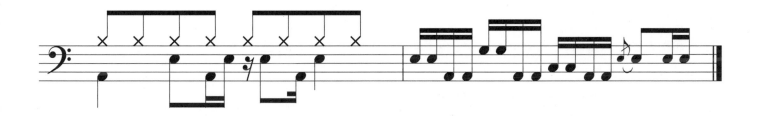

Experiment with the creation of your own 4/4 patterns by combining any 2 x 2/4 patterns with identical hi-hat rhythms.

Try combining different fills with different beats.

SECTION 4

PARADIDDLE PERMUTATIONS

Permutation is the process of changing the starting point of a sequence of numerals or notes in order to discover the possible variations within a particular number or note group. The number of possible permutations is dependant upon the number of numerals or notes within the original sequence.

e.g. The number sequence '1 2 3 4' has 4 possible permutations:

```
1 )   1   2   3   4
2 )   2   3   4   1
3 )   3   4   1   2
4 )   4   1   2   3
```

The paradiddle is a sequence of eight notes. Therefore, the number of possible permutations of a paradiddle is eight:

```
1 )   R   L   R   R   L   R   L   L
2 )   L   R   R   L   R   L   L   R
3 )   R   R   L   R   L   L   R   L
4 )   R   L   R   L   L   R   L   R
5 )   L   R   L   L   R   L   R   R
6 )   R   L   L   R   L   R   R   L
7 )   L   L   R   L   R   R   L   R
8 )   L   R   L   R   R   L   R   L
```

The most commonly used permutations are numbers 3 and 6.

R R L R L L R L

R L L R L R R L

SOLO 20

64.

SOLO 21

65.

If the right hand is moved around the toms in a **clockwise** direction using the sticking pattern of permutation 6, the example below is created.

If the right hand starts again on tom 1 but moves in an **anticlockwise** direction, the example below is created.

SOLO 17

The 8 bar solo below incorporates the previous two examples.

CD 1 **60.**

The example below features accents on the single right hand notes of the sticking.

CD 1 **61.0**

Bass drum and crash cymbal are played on the accented notes below.

CD 1 **61.1**

If the right hand is moved around the toms in a **clockwise** direction using the sticking pattern of permutation 3, the example below is created.

If the right hand starts again on tom 1 but moves in an **anticlockwise** direction, the example below is created.

SOLO 18

The 8 bar solo below incorporates the previous two examples.

 **62.**

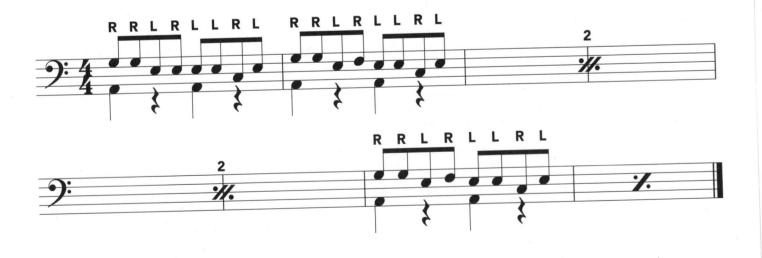

The example below features accents on the single right hand notes

Bass drum and crash cymbal are played on the accented notes belo

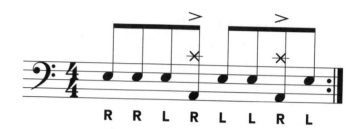

SOLO 19

The following 3 eight bar solos use the paradiddle and two of its pe various fill-ins. All stickings are played as sixteenth notes.

63.

Paradiddles and inversions of (an inversion is another name for a permutation) can be played between bass drum and snare drum.

66.

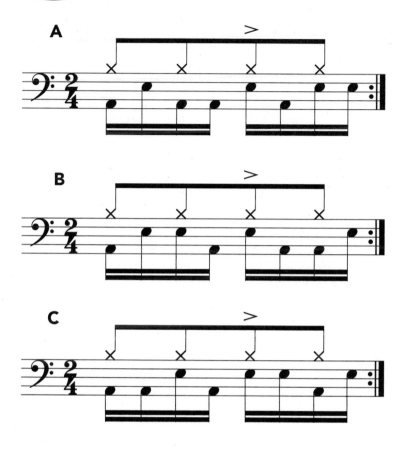

PARADIDDLE PARTIALS

Each of the above examples can be split into 2 one beat **partials**.

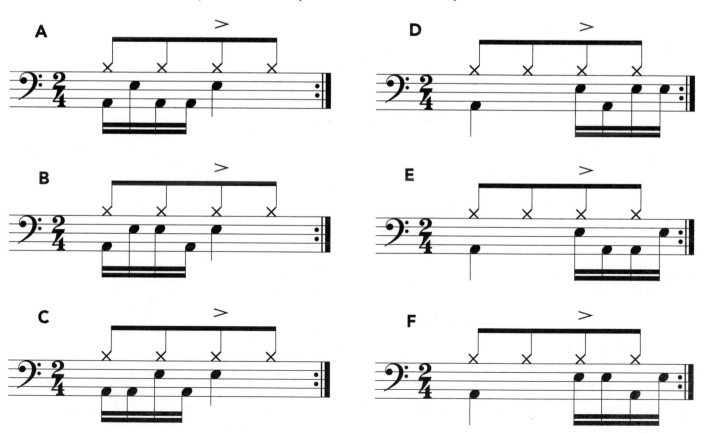

These 1 beat partials can be combined with each other or other rhythmic groupings.

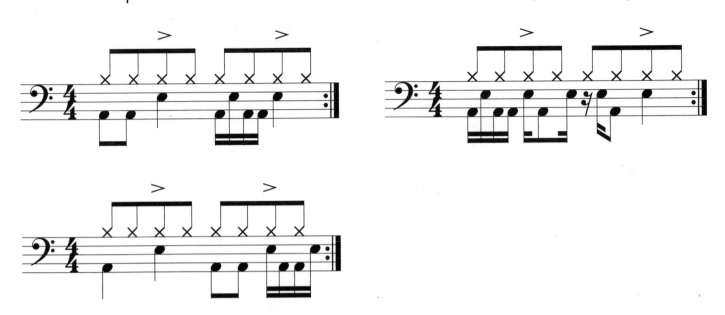

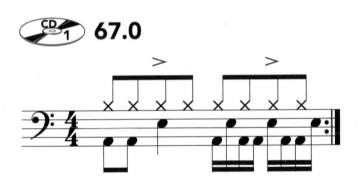

67.0

67.1

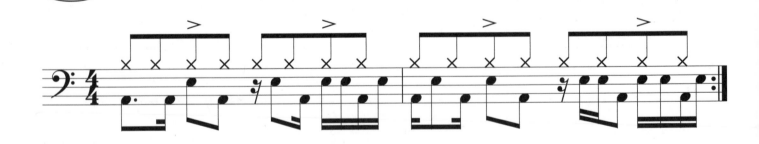

67.2

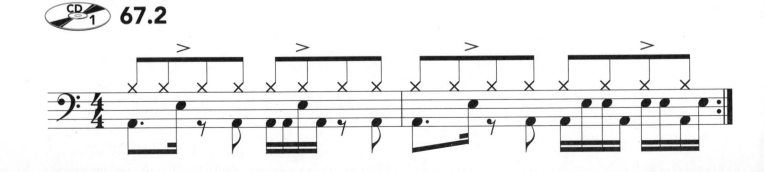

REPETITION COUNTING

There are two different methods of counting, each performing a different function. When learning a new musical idea, the count is dependant upon the notes within that musical idea. e.g.

Count:

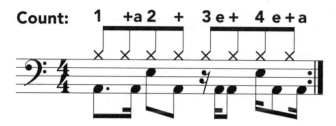

This is a **standard** counting system.

Once comfortable, many repetitions of the musical idea are needed in order to **master** it. Practice is basically a two part process:

    1) Learning

    2) Repetition

Learning requires **standard** counting. Repetition requires **repetition** counting.

Repetition counting, as the name suggests, is a counting system designed to count each repetition of a musical idea. When counting to one hundred there are three differences between repetition counting and the regular numeric counting system:

        1) Seven becomes **'Sen'**

        2) Eleven becomes **'Len'**

        3) Most **'ty'** syllables are omitted

Each of these changes reduces syllables. The reduction in syllables facilitates greater speed and rhythm when counting. Counting thirty bars of $\frac{4}{4}$ time using the repetition counting system would look like this:

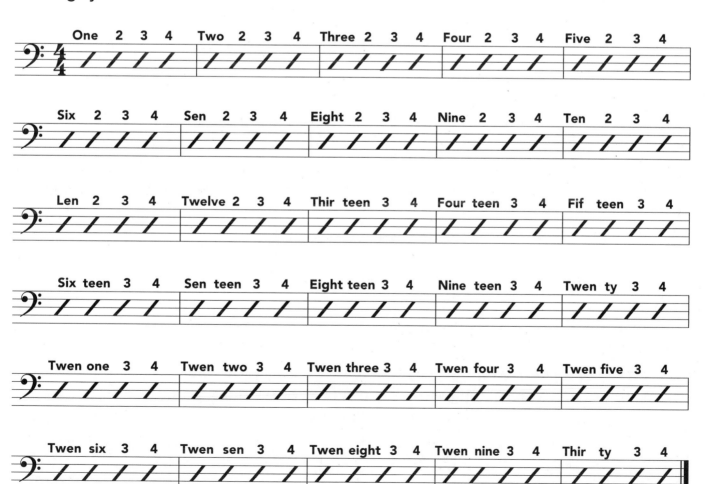

The following features can be seen from the previous page:

- Counting to twelve can be done monosyllabically (using only one syllable).
- From thirteen onwards all number counts use two syllables.
- Each syllable falls on a new quarter note, e.g. | thir - teen 3 4 |
- From twenty onwards, the syllable **'ty'** only appears on the first count of each group of ten.

Counting using one syllable per beat (quarter note) serves two functions:

    i) It allows us to count at a greater speed.
    ii) It instills and reinforces a constant rhythmic quarter note pulse.

Using a maximum of two syllables for all number counts up to one hundred (the one hundredth bar would be counted | hun - dred 3 4 |) allows this counting system usage with **any** time signature, e.g. $\frac{2}{4}, \frac{3}{4}, \frac{4}{4}$ etc.

Counting beyond one hundred is impossible without using a lot of syllables per number count. Bear in mind, in $\frac{4}{4}$ time at a tempo of 60 BPM, counting one hundred repetitions would take 6.666 minutes. However, if multiple lots of one hundred repetitions is required, use the same counting system but keep track of each group of one hundred reps (repetitions) by hitting a different sound source: e.g.

1st	100 - Hi-Hat
2nd	100 - Ride
3rd	100 - Crash
4th	100 - Rim of tom 1etc.

The repetition counting system has the following advantages:

1) The brain sorts by differences. Giving each repetition a different 'name' makes each rep different and also lays down markers of time. This facilitates **greater memory retention**.

2) It instills and reinforces a constant quarter note pulse.

3) It strengthens our level of concentration.

4) It allows us to count at great speed.

5) It adds an extra degree of difficulty to a musical idea, as our brain needs to concentrate on another task. Task splitting the brain into greater divisions forces it to learn a musical idea to the degree where less concentration is needed to execute that idea.

SECTION 5

TRIPLETS

A triplet is a group of three notes played in the same space of time as a group of two notes of the same note type.

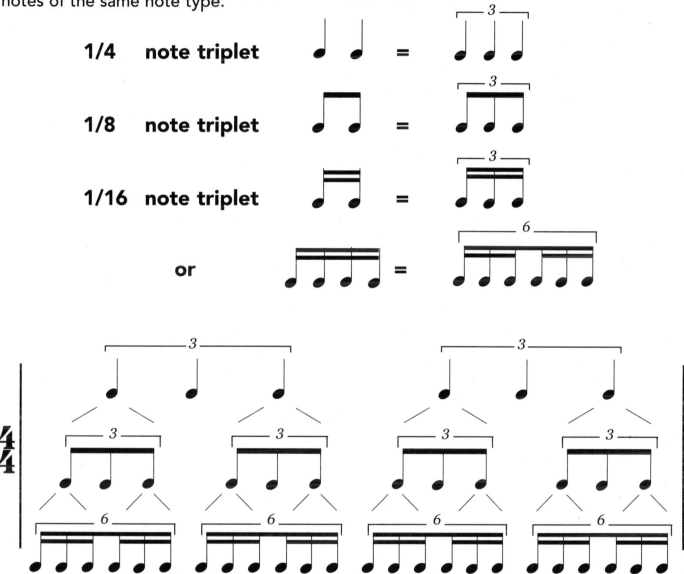

1/4   note triplet

1/8   note triplet

1/16   note triplet

or

Any note grouping whose value is not an even number when divided by two, must have a bracket written over it and indicate the number of notes per group, unless the time signature dictates otherwise.

EIGHTH NOTE TRIPLETS

If we follow the triplet rule it can be seen that there are twelve eighth note triplets in one bar of $\frac{4}{4}$ time.

Count: 1   + ah 2 + ah 3   +   ah 4 + ah

1 bar rhythmic variations featuring the rhythmic figures ♩ and

 **1.0**

1 + a 2 + a 3 + a 4 + a

SIGHT READING EXERCISE 19

16 bar sight reading exercise featuring the rhythmic figures ♩ and ♪♪♪ .

Eighth note triplets are played on the hi-hat in the following examples.

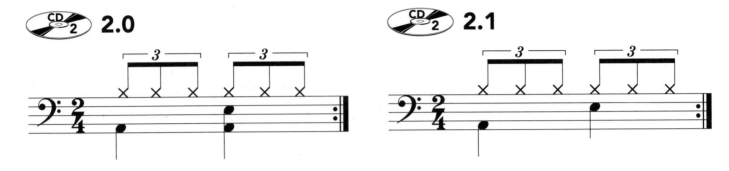

Here are 3 different fills using the eighth note triplet.

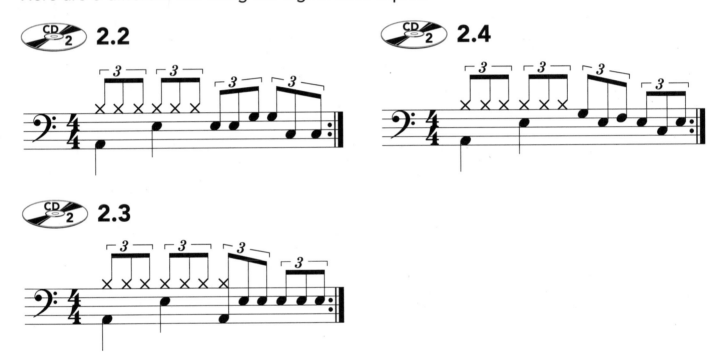

The fill below introduces the **Paradiddle-diddle** sticking.

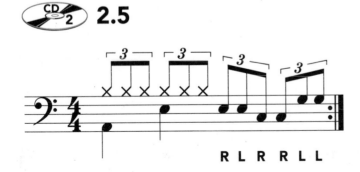

R L R R L L

Rhythmic variations for snare drum and or bass drum featuring the rhythmic figure.

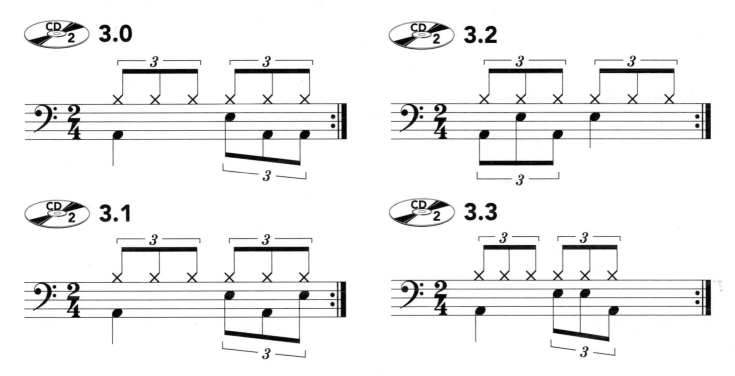

3.0

3.2

3.1

3.3

1 bar variations.

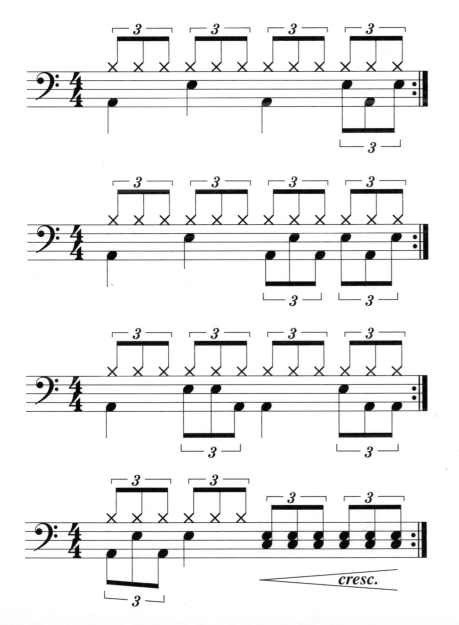

cresc.

SOLO 22

 **4.**

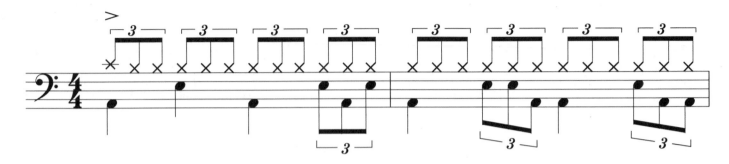

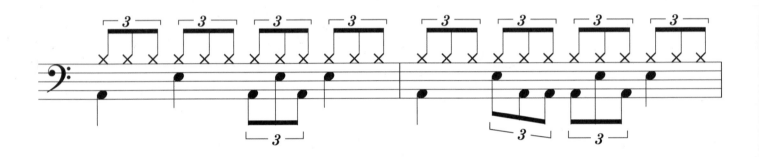

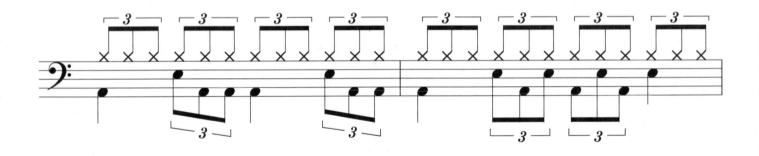

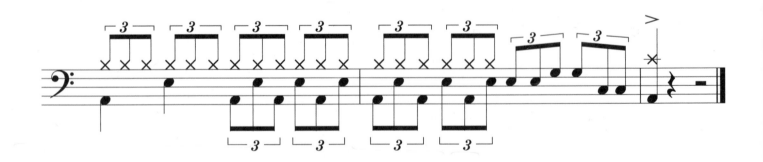

THE EIGHTH NOTE TRIPLET REST

This is an eighth note triplet rest and indicates silence for the count of one eighth note triplet. It is the same as an eighth note rest, but functions as a triplet rest in the context of eighth note triplets.

INTRODUCING THE RHYTHMIC FIGURE

1 bar rhythmic variations featuring the rhythmic figures  and .

5.

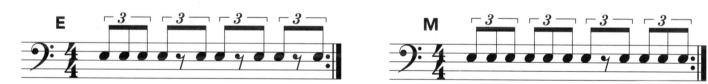

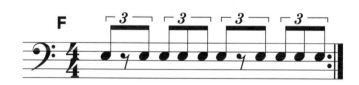

SIGHT READING EXERCISE 20

16 bar sight reading exercise featuring the rhythmic figures  and .

Rhythmic variations for snare and or bass drum featuring the rhythmic figure and previously covered rhythmic figures.

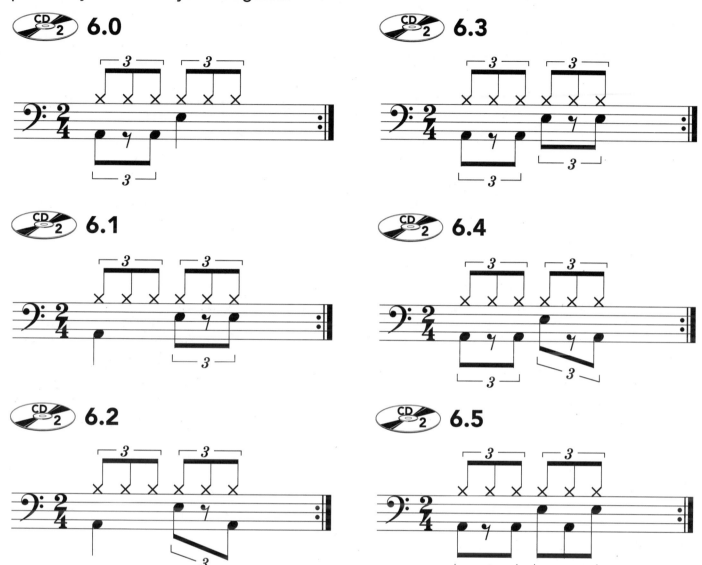

1 bar variations.

114

SOLO 23

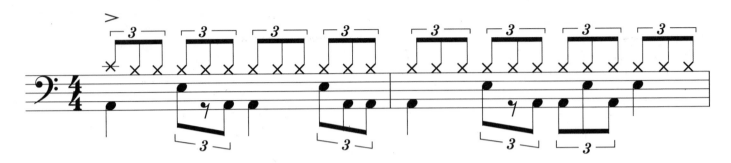

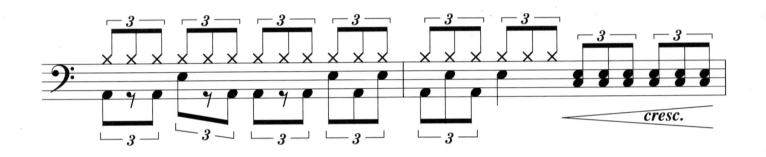

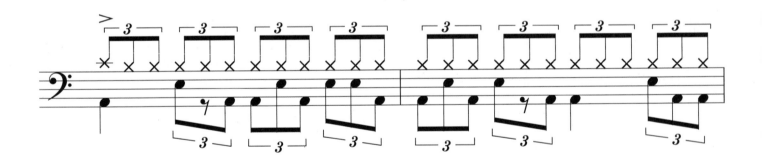

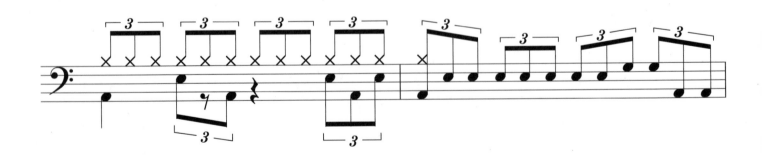

SHUFFLE RHYTHM

The **shuffle** is a common rhythmic variation based upon the triplet. It is created by omitting the middle note of the triplet, as indicated by the tie.

Count: 1   a 2   a 3   a 4   a

This can also be written as:

or

A pattern is said to have a **shuffle** feel when the above rhythm is played on cymbal or between any two sound sources e.g. kick and snare.

Rhythmic variations for snare and or bass drum are combined with a shuffle rhythm hi-hat pattern in the examples on the following page.

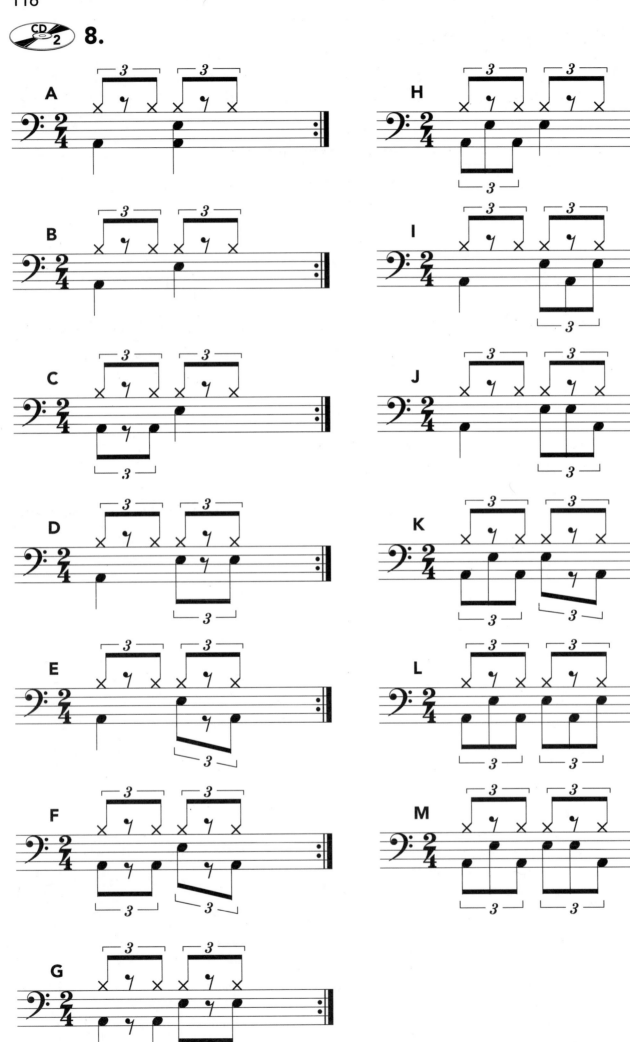

1 bar variations.

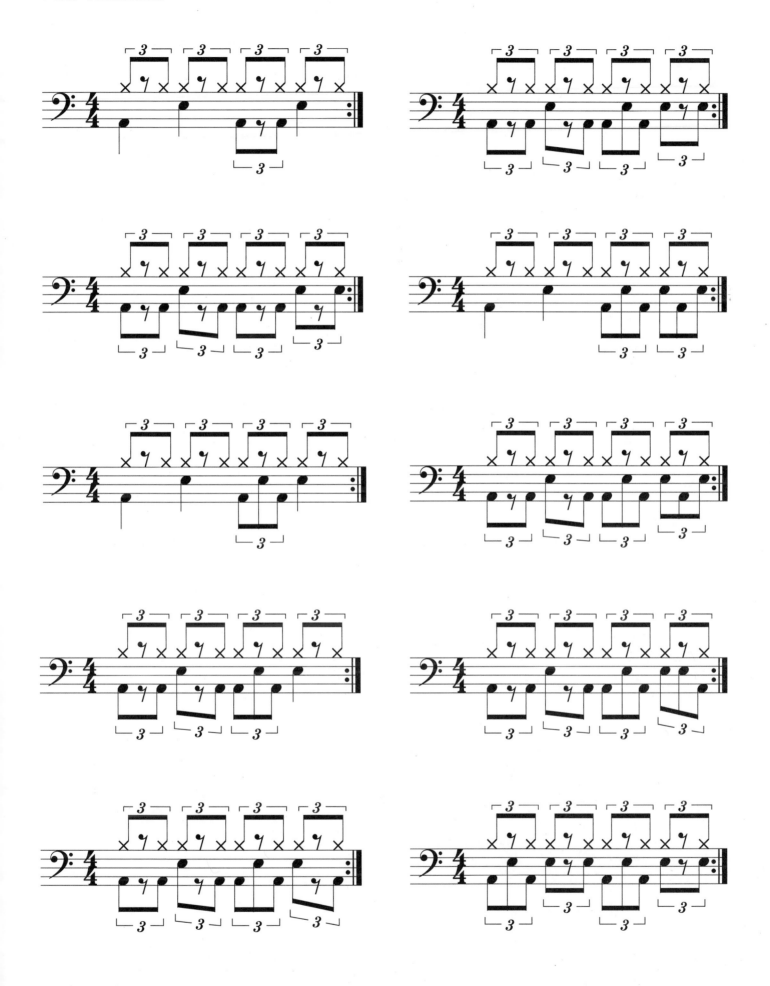

SOLO 24

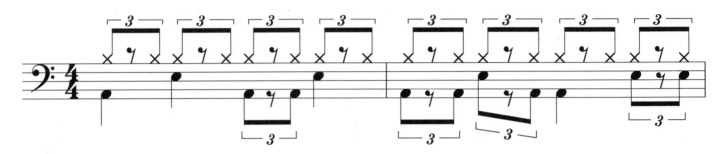

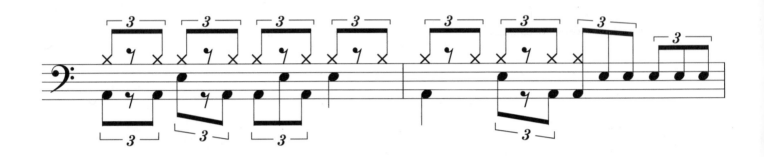

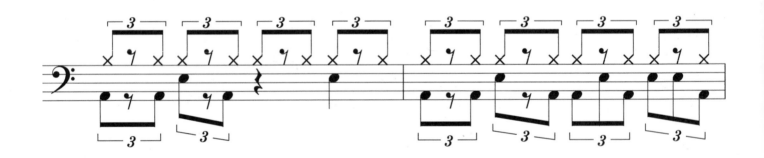

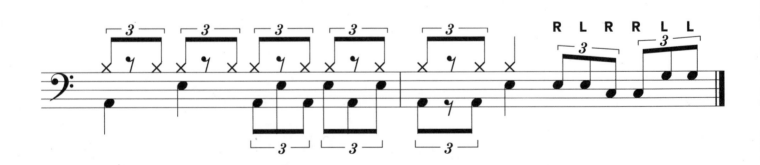

SWING RHYTHM

The **swing** rhythm is another commonly used rhythmic variation based upon the triplet. It is used primarily in **Jazz** music and differs from the shuffle rhythm through its use of quarter notes on beats 1 and 3.

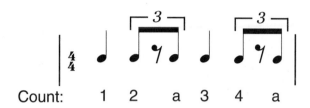

The ride cymbal is the rhythmic foundation for most jazz drumming.
Below are three simple jazz patterns all featuring the swing rhythm on ride cymbal and a foot closed hi-hat on beats 2 and 4.

10.0

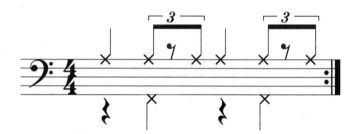

10.1

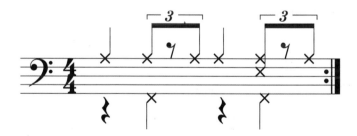

10.2

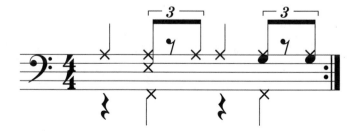

120

INTRODUCING THE RHYTHMIC FIGURE

1 bar rhythmic variations featuring the rhythmic figures and .

11.

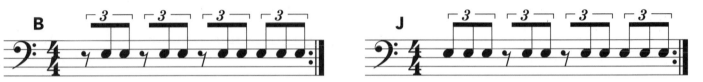

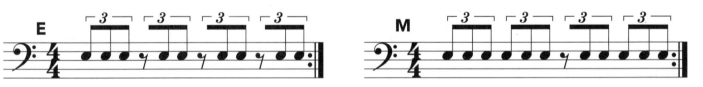

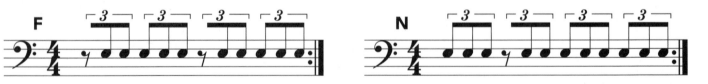
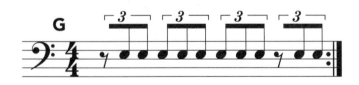
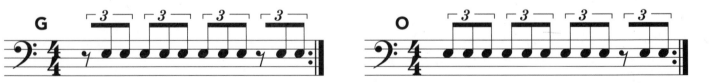

SIGHT READING EXERCISE 21

16 bar sight reading exercise featuring the rhythmic figures ♪♪♪ and ♪♪♪.

Rhythmic variations for snare and or bass drum featuring the rhythmic figure ♪♫♩ and previously covered rhythmic figures.

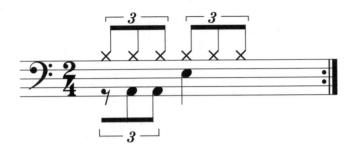

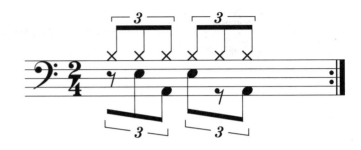

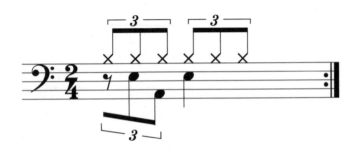

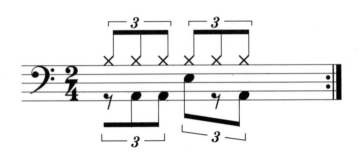

 **12.0**

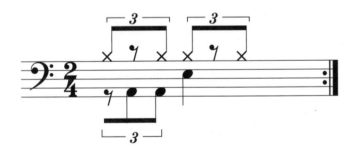

 **12.2**

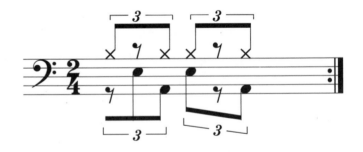

 **12.1**

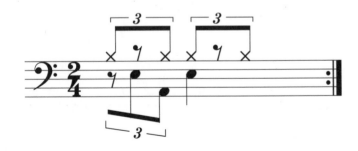

12.3

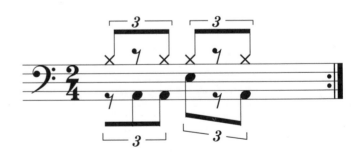

1 bar variations.

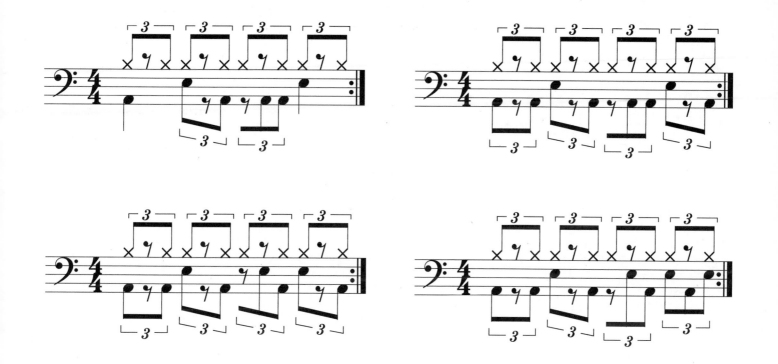

SOLO 25

 **13.**

INTRODUCING THE RHYTHMIC FIGURE

1 bar rhythmic variations featuring the rhythmic figures  and .

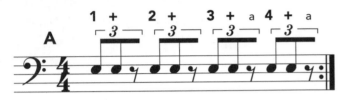

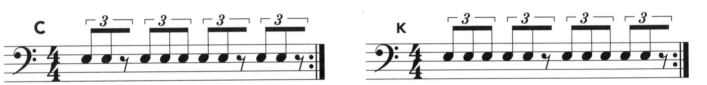

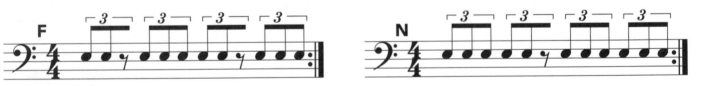

SIGHT READING EXERCISE 22

16 bar sight reading exercise featuring the rhythmic figures and .

126

Rhythmic variations for bass drum featuring the rhythmic figure and previously covered rhythmic figures.

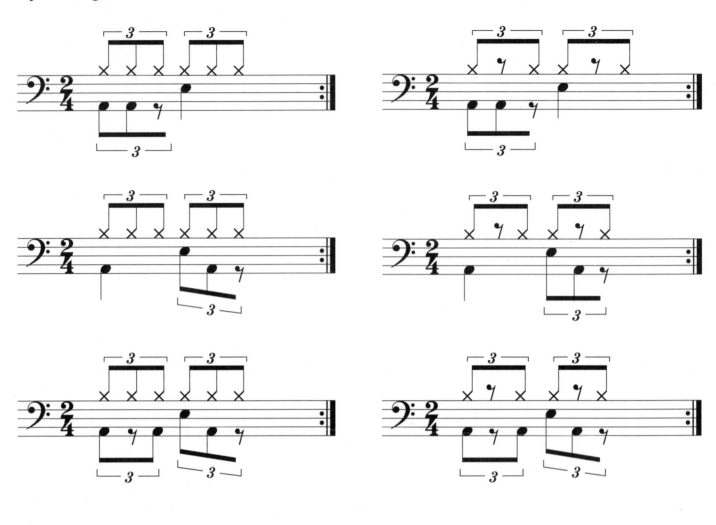

1 bar variations.

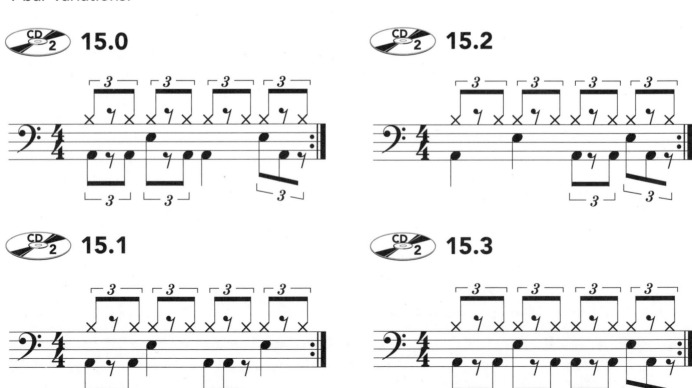

SOLO 26

The following fill-ins incorporate bass drum.

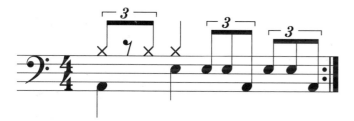

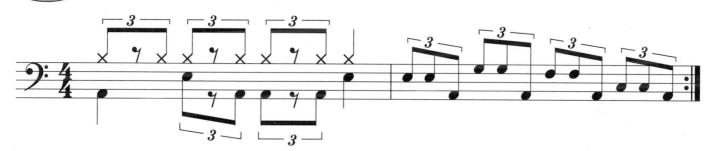

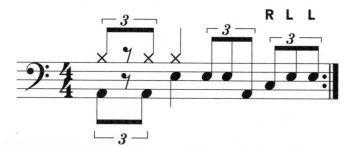

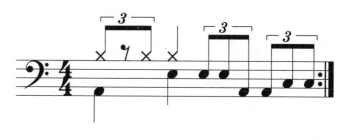

INTRODUCING THE RHYTHMIC FIGURE

1 bar rhythmic variations featuring the rhythmic figures and .

17.

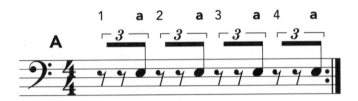

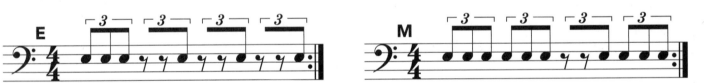

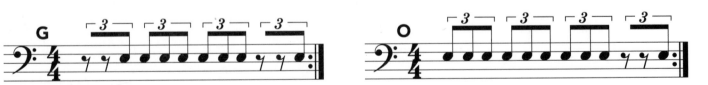

SIGHT READING EXERCISE 23

16 bar sight reading exercise featuring the rhythmic figures ♪♪♪ and ♪♪♪.

INTRODUCING THE RHYTHMIC FIGURE

1 bar rhythmic variations featuring the rhythmic figures and .

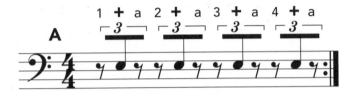

SIGHT READING EXERCISE 24

16 bar sight reading exercise featuring the rhythmic figures and .

Rhythmic variations for bass drum featuring the rhythmic figures and .

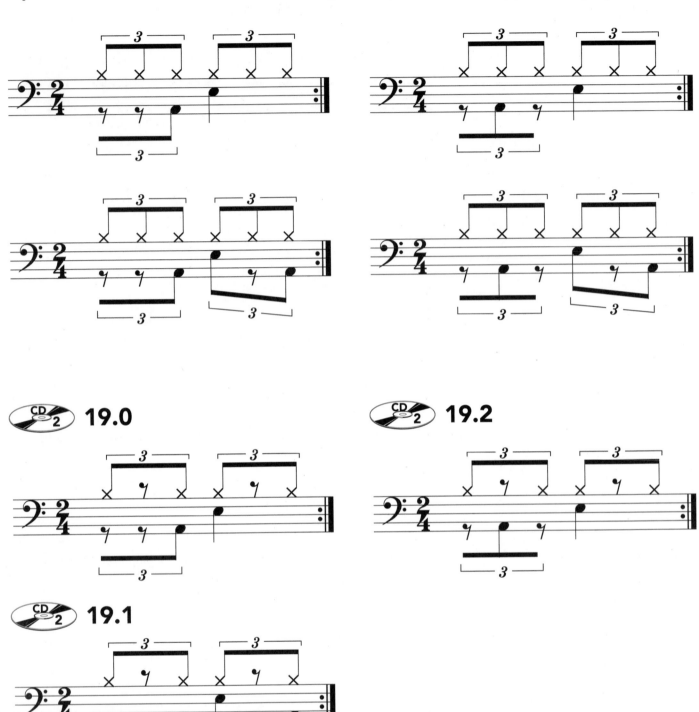

1 bar variations.

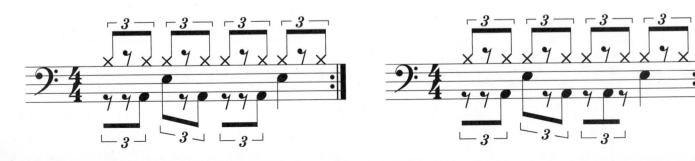

SOLO 27

– Experiment with the creation of your own $\frac{4}{4}$ patterns by combining any 2 x $\frac{2}{4}$ patterns with identical hi-hat rhythms.

– Try combining different fills with different beats.

THE QUARTER NOTE TRIPLET

Following the triplet rule (page 105), three quarter note triplets are played in the same space of time as two quarter notes. Therefore there are 6 quarter note triplets in 1 bar of $\frac{4}{4}$ time.

Count: **1** + **ah** 2 + ah **3** + **ah** 4 + ah

THE QUARTER NOTE TRIPLET REST

This is a quarter note triplet rest and indicates silence for the count of one quarter note triplet.

1 bar rhythmic variations featuring the rhythmic figure  and previously covered triplet rhythmic figures.

21.

A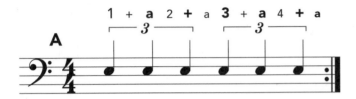

H

B

I

C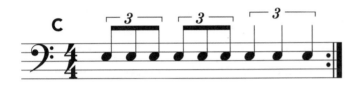

J

D

K

E

L

F

M

G

Play **A** to **M** without repeats.

INTRODUCING THE RHYTHMIC FIGURE

1 bar rhythmic variations featuring the rhythmic figure and previously covered triplet rhythmic figures.

22.

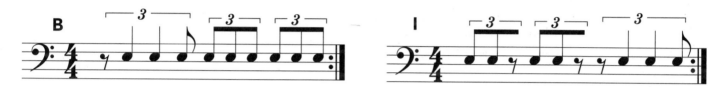

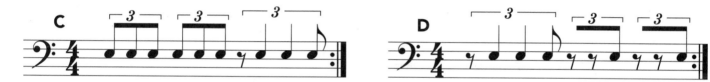

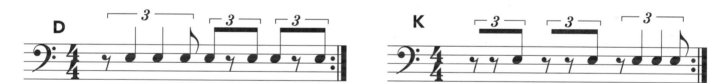

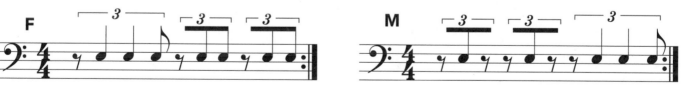

Play **A** to **M** without repeats.

Quarter note triplets feature in the following examples.

 **23.0**

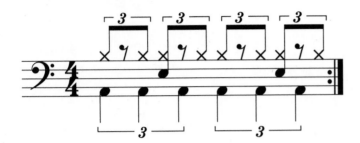

 **23.1**

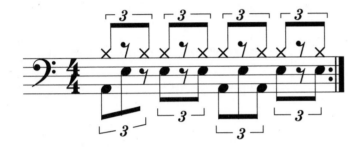

 **23.2**

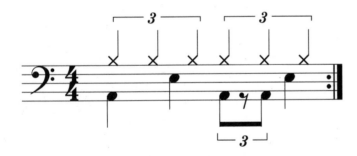

SOLO 28

SIXTEENTH NOTE TRIPLETS

Following the triplet rule (page 105), three sixteenth note triplets are played in the same space of time as two sixteenth notes. Therefore there are 24 sixteenth note triplets in 1 bar of $\frac{4}{4}$ time.

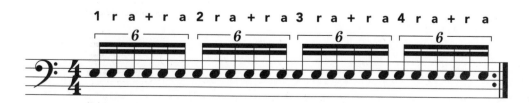

Note: 'r' is pronounced 'er'.

138

1 bar rhythmic variations featuring the rhythmic figures and .

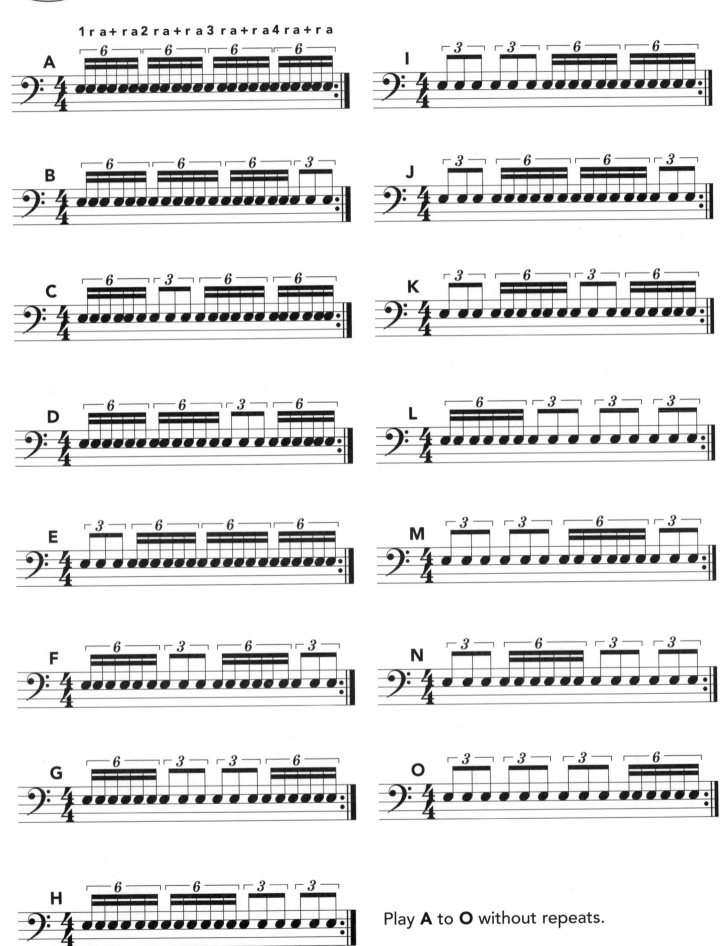

Play **A** to **O** without repeats.

SIGHT READING EXERCISE 25

16 bar sight reading exercise featuring the rhythmic figures ♪♪♪ and ♪♪♪♪♪♪ .

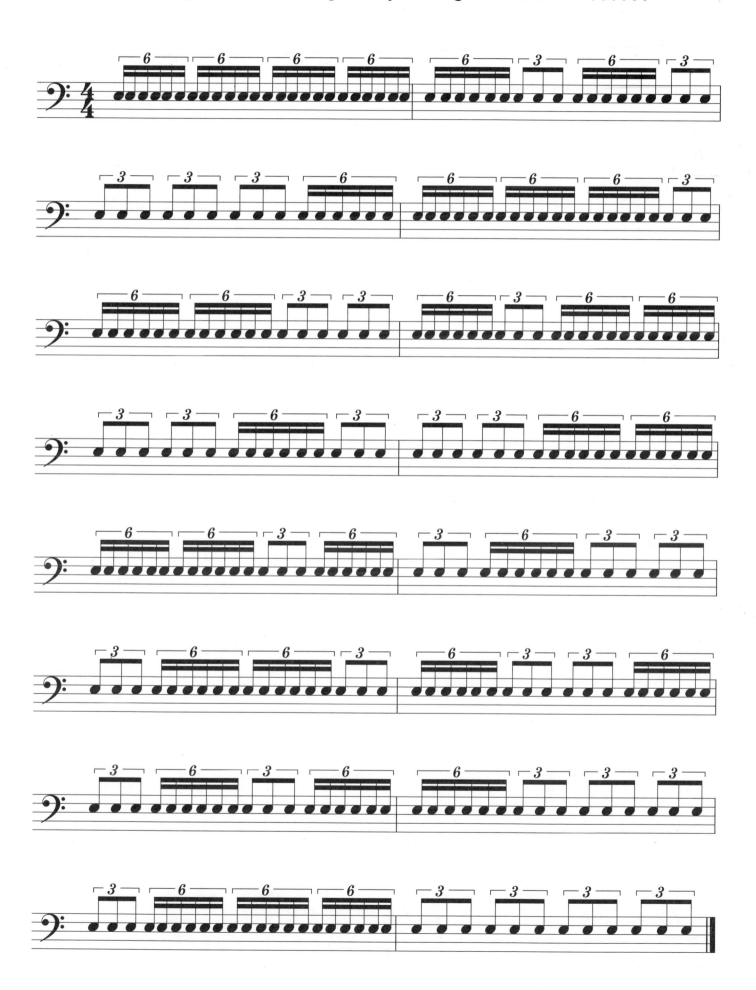

INTRODUCING THE RHYTHMIC FIGURES  and .

1 bar rhythmic variations featuring and . There are no brackets above the triplets here, but this makes no difference to the duration of the notes.

26.

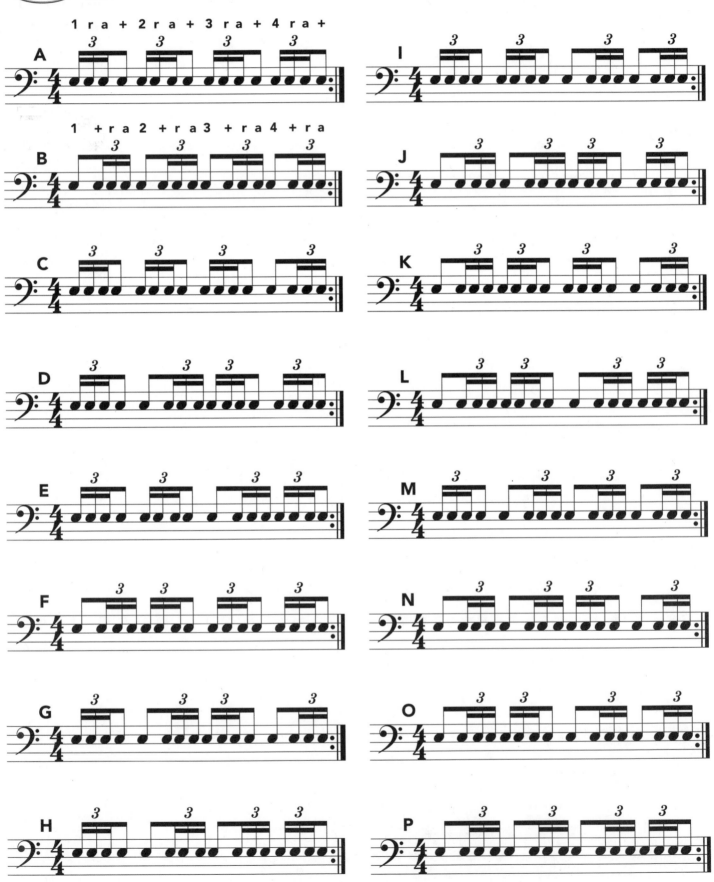

Play **A** to **P** without repeats.

The following fill-ins feature the sixteenth note triplet.

27.0

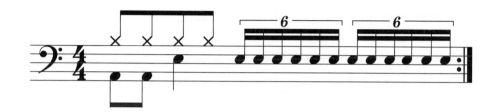

27.1

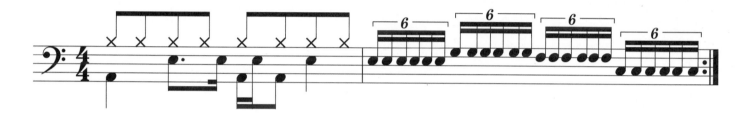

27.2

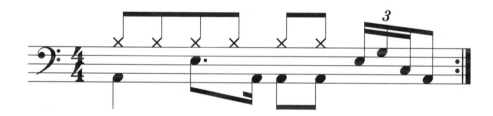

27.3

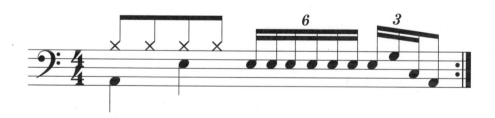

27.4

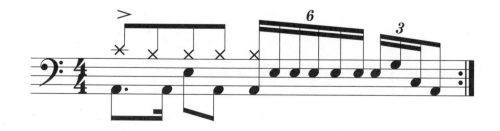

THE $\frac{12}{8}$ FEEL

The term '$\frac{12}{8}$ feel' refers to the action of playing 12 eighth notes on hi-hat or ride cymbal at a relatively slow tempo. These 12 eighth notes can be thought of as eighth note triplets in $\frac{4}{4}$ time, or a bar of $\frac{12}{8}$ time.

$\frac{12}{8}$ time places emphasis on four dotted quarter notes.

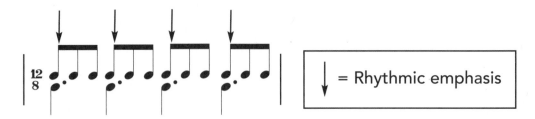

Any time signature which places rhythmic emphasis on a dotted note is referred to as **compound time**.

Here is a pattern written in $\frac{4}{4}$ and $\frac{12}{8}$ time.

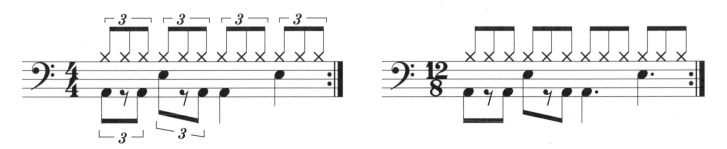

Both written versions sound identical. Both can be said to have a '$\frac{12}{8}$ feel'.
The main advantage of writing $\frac{12}{8}$ time is the omission of the triplet symbols.

'SWINGING' A PATTERN

Any straight pattern (eighth notes and sixteenth notes) can be swung if the offbeats are interpreted as the third beat of each triplet grouping

e.g. ♫ becomes ♪♪ and ♬ becomes ♪♪.

Using eighth notes, only the '**+**'s are affected. Using sixteenth notes, the '**e**'s and '**a**'s are affected.

Original Version

🔘 **28.0**

Swung Version

🔘 **28.1**

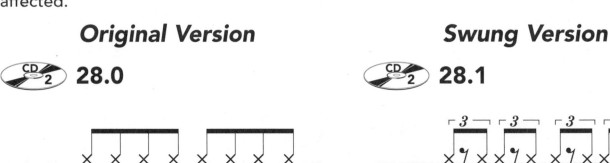

28.2 Original Version

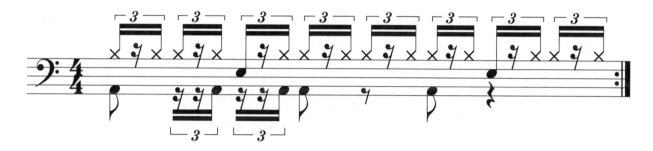

28.3 Swung Version

28.4 Original Version

28.5 Swung Version

Try 'swinging' any of the straight patterns previously covered.

The following examples have a $\frac{12}{8}$ feel and feature various ways of using the sixteenth note triplet.

29.0

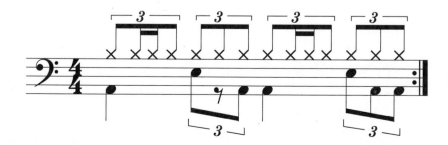

29.1

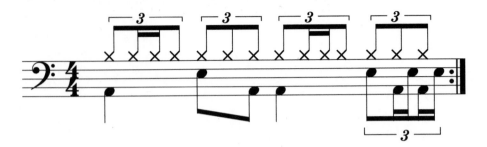

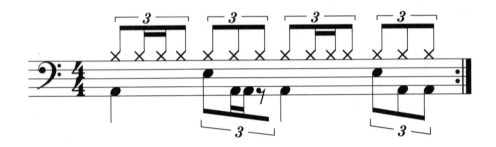

29.2

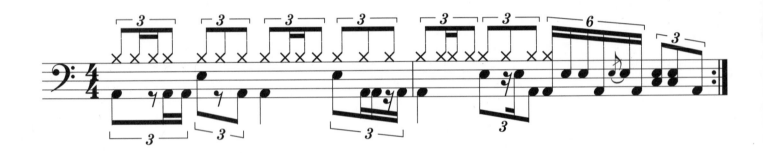

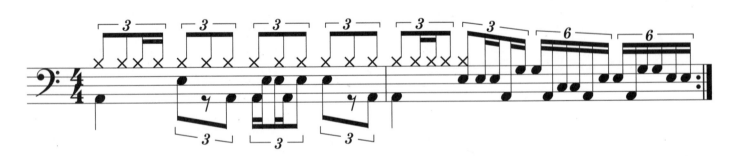

This example features a swung interpretation of the sixteenth note triplets.

29.3

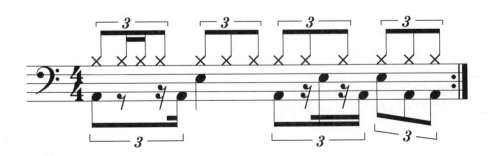

SECTION 6

RUDIMENTS

Rudiments (also called sticking[s]) are sticking exercises which vary the combinations of left and right hand movements. They are designed to achieve the following:

1) Improve stick control - and hence expand the possibilities of speed, dynamics and uniformity (evenness).
2) Facilitate greater ease when playing. Potentially difficult ideas become easier when the correct sticking is chosen.
3) Improve rhythmic possibilities. Different stickings create different rhythmic effects. Such rhythmic possibilities increase again when a sticking is played between two or more sound sources.

When playing rudiments:

1) Use a metronome.
2) Keep a continuous quarter note pulse by either tapping the right foot or playing the bass drum as written.
3) Vary the dynamics (page 14 explains in detail).
4) Vary the tempo.
5) Vary the sticking by starting with either the right or left hand.
6) Play with and without written accents.

Practicing rudiments can become boring if you let it, so coming up with ideas to prevent this is a good policy. Practicing rudiments along with a recording is one such idea.

ADAPTING TIME SIGNATURES

Some rudiments written in traditional form may look unusable because the time signatures used are $\frac{2}{4}$ and $\frac{6}{8}$. These time signatures can be easily adapted to $\frac{4}{4}$ time.

If a $\frac{2}{4}$ bar is played twice, the effect is the same as playing one bar of $\frac{4}{4}$ time.

If each of the notes in a $\frac{6}{8}$ bar is treated as the corresponding triplet of a $\frac{4}{4}$ bar, $\frac{4}{4}$ time can be formulated e.g.

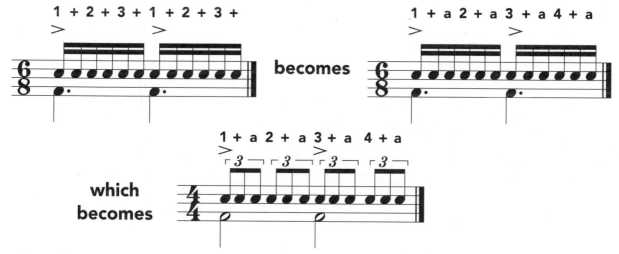

Note: Time Signatures are explained on pages 12, 31 and 142.

A $\frac{4}{4}$ version of the traditionally notated $\frac{6}{8}$ rudiments has been included where applicable.

'DIDDLE' RUDIMENTS

 30.0 Single Stroke   R1

 30.1 Double Stroke   R2

 30.2 Paradiddle   R3

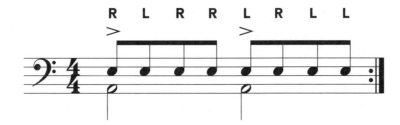

 30.3 Double Paradiddle   R4

or

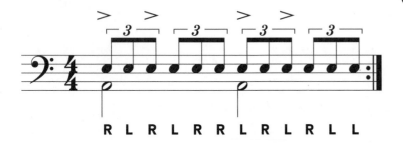

30.4 Triple Paradiddle   R5

30.5 Paradiddle-diddle   R6

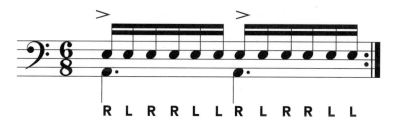

or

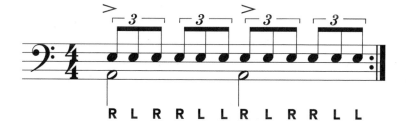

FLAM RUDIMENTS

 30.6 Flam   R7

 30.7 Flam Tap   R8

30.8 Flam Paradiddle   R9

 31.0 Flamacue   R10

31.1 Inverted Flam Tap   R11

 31.2 Pataflafla   R12

 31.3 Single Flammed Mill   R13

31.4 Flam Accent   R14

or

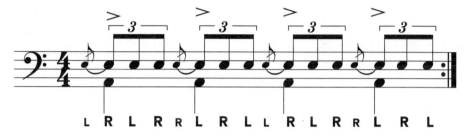

31.5 Flam Paradiddle-diddle   R15

or

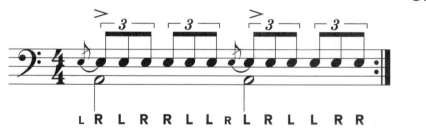

31.6 Swiss Army Triplet   R16

31.7 Flam Drag   R17

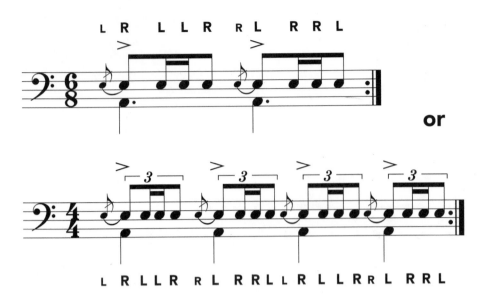

or

DRAG, RATAMACUE AND RUFF RUDIMENTS

31.8 Drag   R18

31.9 Single Drag Tap   R19

32.0 Single Dragadiddle   R20

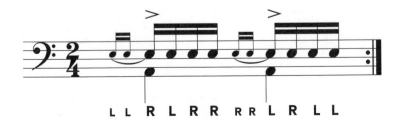

32.1 Drag Paradiddle 1   R21

R LL R L R R L rr L R L L

or

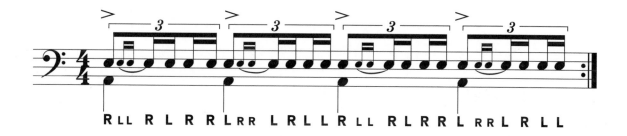

R LL R L R R L rr L R L L R LL R L R R L rr L R L L

32.2 Drag Paradiddle 2   R22

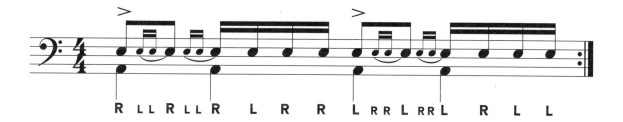

R LL R LL R L R R L rr L rr L R L L

32.3 Double Drag Tap   R23

LL R LL R L rr L rr L R

or

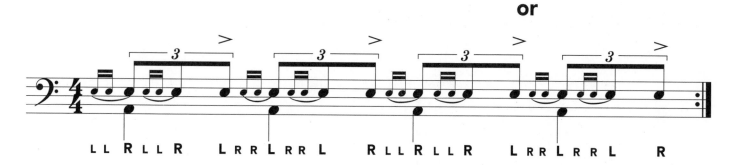

LL R LL R L rr L rr L R LL R LL R L rr L rr L R

32.4 Drag Tap Tap   R24

 32.5 Single Ratamacue   R25

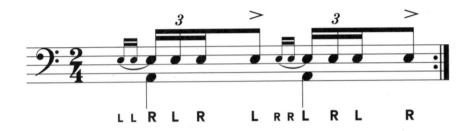

 32.6 Double Ratamacue   R26

or

32.7 Triple Ratamacue **R27**

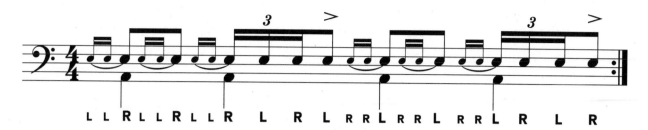

 32.8 Four Stroke Ruff **R28**

THIRTY SECOND NOTES

There are 32 thirty second notes in one bar of $\frac{4}{4}$ time, or 8 thirty second notes per beat.

 **33.0**

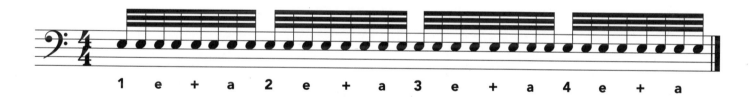

SIXTY FOURTH NOTES

There are 64 sixty fourth notes in one bar of $\frac{4}{4}$ time, or 16 sixty fourth notes per beat.

 **33.1**

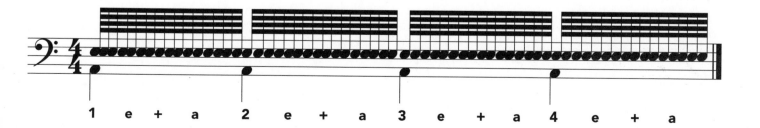

ROLLS

Rolls originated in military and traditional bands and are used to give the effect of a sustained note. Many of the rolls have an abbreviated form which is used to condense the written form of rolls on the staff and hence simplify reading. Many of the rolls which follow are written in abbreviated form and common notation form.

 33.2 Single Stroke Roll   (same sticking as R1)

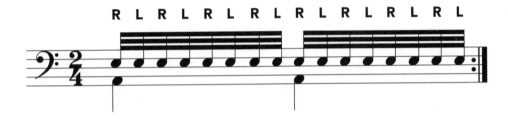

 33.3 Single Stroke Four   **R29**

 33.4 Single Stroke Seven   **R30**

 33.5 Multiple Bounce Roll   **R31**

Finger pressure (from pinky, ring and middle fingers) extracts multiple bounces from one downstroke.

33.6 Triple Stroke Roll **R32**

 33.7 Double Stroke Open Roll (same sticking as R2)

or

← Common Notation Form

 33.8 Five Stroke Roll **R33**

or

33.9 Six Stroke Roll 1   R34

 34.0 Six Stroke Roll 2   R35

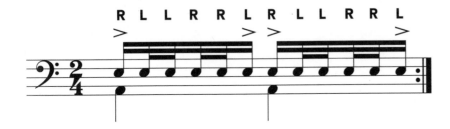

 34.1 Seven Stroke Roll   R36

34.2 Nine Stroke Roll   R37

34.3 Ten Stroke Roll   R38

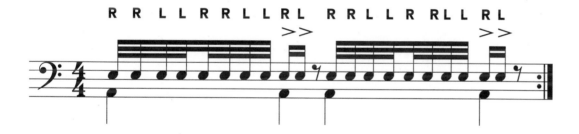

34.4 Eleven Stroke Roll   R39

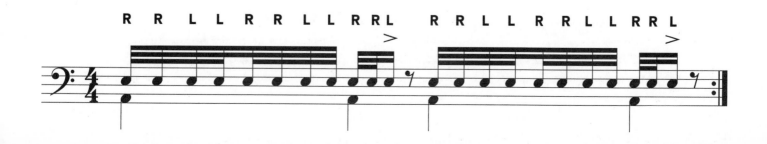

158

 34.5 Thirteen Stroke Roll   R40

 34.6 Fifteen Stoke Roll   R41

 34.7 Seventeen Stroke Roll   R42

STICKINGS AROUND THE KIT

1) Practice a specific sticking on a practice pad or snare drum until comfortable.

2) Play the sticking with the right and left hands on two different sound sources.

3) Move the right and left hands randomly between two or more sound sources, experimenting with your own ideas.

4) Use some of the resultant ideas as fills (an explanation of fills is on page 19) and make them part of your vocabulary.

5) Repeat steps 1-4 using a new sticking.

6) Repeat steps 1-4 using combinations of two or more stickings.

The following are examples of some of the steps listed above using the single stroke sticking.

Step 2 (one possibility)

Step 3 (one possibility)

Step 4 (one possibility)

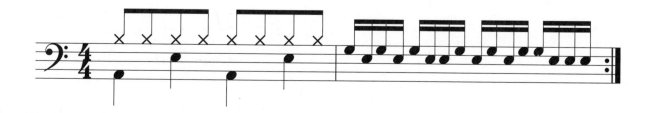

JOINING STICKINGS TOGETHER

1) Practice stickings on a practice pad or snare drum until comfortable.

2) Join two different stickings together over two bars (one bar for each sticking), making sure the transition is smooth and accurate.

3) Join two different stickings together over one bar (two beats for each sticking), again making sure the transition is smooth and accurate.

4) Swap between the two stickings at random until you can swap between the two at any point you desire.

5) Move the right and left hands randomly between two or more sound sources experimenting with your own ideas.

6) Use some of the resultant ideas as fills and make them part of your vocabulary.

7) Repeat steps 1-6 using two new stickings.

8) Practice changing between many different stickings.

The following are examples of some of the steps listed above using the single stroke and double stroke stickings.

Step 2 (one possibility)

Step 3 (one possibility)

Step 4 (one possibility)

Step 5 (one possibility)

Step 6 (one possibility)

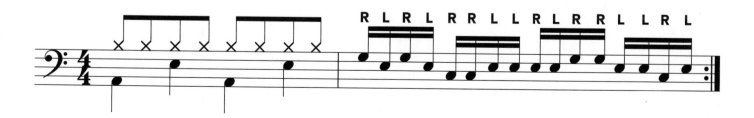

STICKING INTERPRETATION

There are **16** sticking possibilities over **4 events** (4 x 1/4 notes or 4 x 1/8 notes or 4 x 1/16 notes etc). Most sticking are combinations of these 16, so it is important to master each one individually before joining two or more together.

The examples below are written as eighth notes.

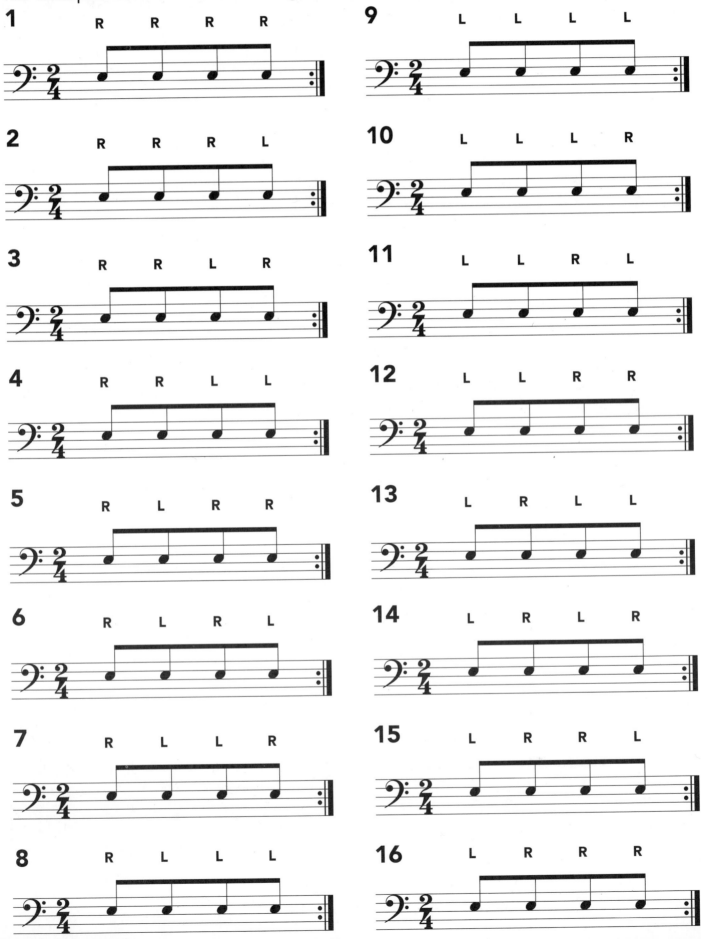

The sticking below is a combination of examples 7 and 11 from the previous page, written as sixteenth notes.

7   **11** ← **sticking possibility**

The following example is the result of steps 3 and 4 from 'stickings around the kit' on page 159.

The bass drum is played in unison with the hi-hat (right hand) in the example below. This is a very commonly used technique. Any cymbal can be substituted for hi-hat e.g. crash or ride.

This example places accents on 2 of the notes of the sticking pattern:

The 4 bar groove below incorporates the previous 3 examples.

35.

Another commonly used sticking interpretation involves substituting both hands in unison for **'R'** and bass drum for **'L'**. The first 3 beats of the pattern below use the aforementioned interpretation.

36.

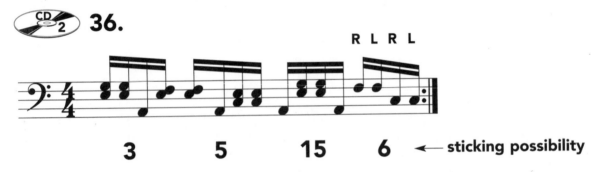

3   **5**   **15**   **6**   ← **sticking possibility**

Here is the above example incorporated into a 4 bar groove.

Experiment with your own sticking interpretation patterns using the ideas below.

1) Join two or more of the 16 sticking possibilities together.

2) Incorporate tom toms using 'Sticking Around the Kit', page 159.

3) Bass drum and cymbal (could be hi-hat, ride or crash) substitute for **'R'**.

4) Experiment with accents.

5) Both hands in unison substitute for **'R'**, bass drum substitutes for **'L'**.

TRIPLET STICKING INTERPRETATION

There are **8** sticking possibilities over **3 events** (3 x 1/4 note triplets or 3 x 1/16 note triplets etc.). Triplet sticking are combinations of these 8.
The examples below are written as one beat of eighth note triplet.

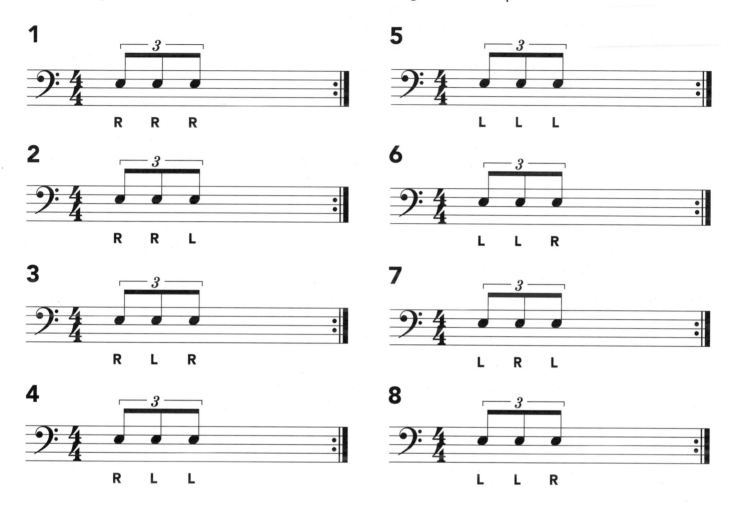

The sticking below is a combination of examples 3, 6, 7 and 4 from the previous page.

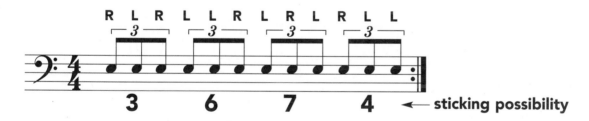

The following example is the result of steps 3 and 4 from 'Stickings Around the Kit' on page 159. Hi-hat and kick are played in unison on beat 1 to create greater rhythmic tension.

The bass drum is played in unison with the hi-hat (right hand) in the example below.

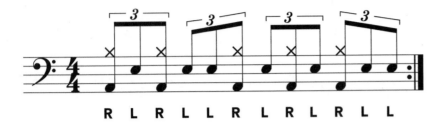

R L R L L R L R L R L L

This example places accents on 3 of the notes of the sticking pattern.

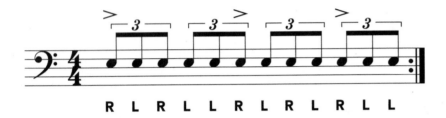

R L R L L R L R L R L L

This 4 bar groove incorporates two of the previous three examples.

 **37.0**

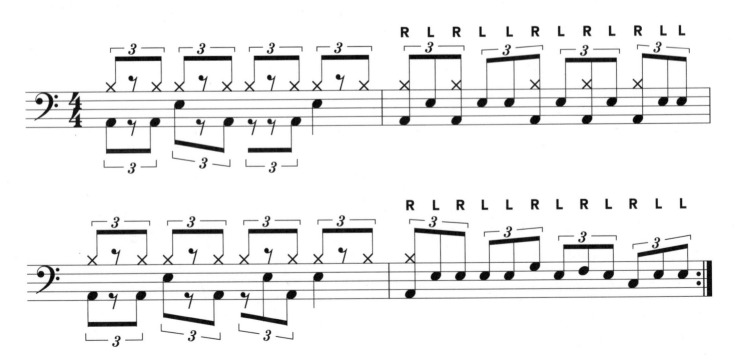

Over the first 3 beats of this example, both hands substitute for 'R' whilst bass drum substitutes for **'L'**.

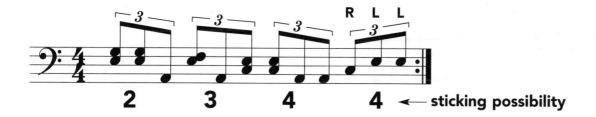

Two of the previous three examples are incorporated into this 4 bar groove.

 **37.1**

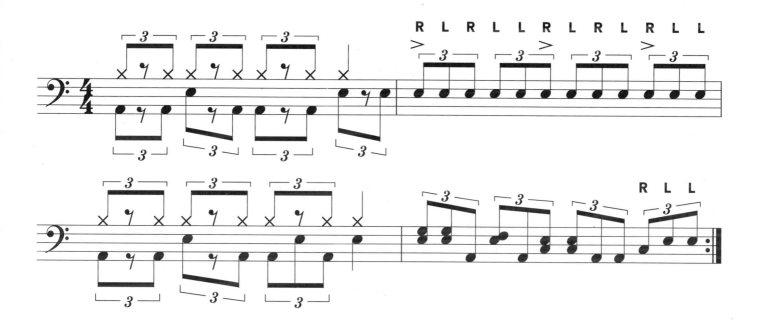

Experiment with your own triplets sticking interpretation patterns using the ideas below.

1) Join two or more of the 8 triplet sticking possibilities together.

2) Incorporate tom toms using 'Stickings Around the Kit', page 159.

3) Bass drum and cymbal substitute for **'R'**.

4) Experiment with accents.

5) Both hands in unison substitute for **'R'**, bass drum substitutes for **'L'**.

SECTION 7

HOW TO PRACTICE

The human brain acts like an advanced tape recorder, capable of recording information on every sensory level, including kinesthetic (feeling, emotion). It is capable of **recording** and **recalling** vast amounts of information. Knowing what factors affect the RECORD/RECALL response greatly improves our learning ability.

The recall percentage is dependant upon the **importance** of the information. The level of importance of information is dependant upon its **frequency, duration** and **intensity**. Intensity is increased by thoroughly understanding:

1) **WHY** - Why a task is performed, why this information is **relevant**.
2) **WHAT** - The actual data or information.
3) **HOW** - How to **use** the information.
4) **WHAT IF** - Experimentation, modifying an idea/information, or combining it with other ideas/information.

3 basic factors affect the RECORD/RECALL response:

1) REPETITION - Practice is repetition. Here are some useful tips on practice:

(i) Because the brain sorts by difference it is beneficial to make each repetition unique. Giving each repetition a different number count means that the brain codes each repetition as unique by way of association. This process greatly improves retention. (Counting is covered in detail on pages 103 and 104).

(ii) Understanding the HOW, WHAT, WHY, WHAT IF, of all practice material.

(iii) New learning takes place **outside** of the **comfort zone**. The trick here is to make the task continually challenging, but not impossible to repeat without mistakes.
Some ways of pushing the comfort zone are:

a) Vary the TEMPO
- As slowly as possible
- As quickly as possible

b) Vary the DYNAMICS
- As quietly as possible
- As loudly as possible

c) Change the rhythm of one limb or add one limb e.g. foot closed hi-hat.

d) Combine different ideas together e.g. different beats with different fills.

2) EVALUATION - Evaluation occurs during an exercise (e.g. are all unison voices exactly together? or where am I storing tension?) and after an exercise (e.g. I need to work on softer dynamics or relaxation at higher tempos).

3) INTEGRATION - The brain continues to process information after an exercise is completed. This is why practicing for 30 minutes in the morning and 30 minutes in the afternoon is more effective than a 1 hour session once a day.

- How and what is practiced determines how and what is recalled. Therefore practicing SLOWLY and PRECISELY is most effective.

- The formula for speed is PRECISION plus REPETITION.

- The greater the degree of concentration on as many levels as possible, the greater the RECORD/RECALL response.

Other factors requiring focused attention:
1) Relaxation - Systematically search for any tension spots. Focus your attention on the muscles which are unnecessarily tense and work toward relaxing them. Tensing the affected muscle before trying to achieve a greater level of relaxation can be effective.

2) Dynamics - Overall and between each limb and or sound source.

3) Feel - Is your timing accurate? Are any sound sources stylistically ahead or behind the beat? What feel are you trying to create?

4) Balance Point - Minor adjustments to body position can have a great impact on your ability to move each limb freely and independently.

5) Sound - Is the sound crisp and clean? Minor adjustments to technique can have a great impact on the sound you extract from the drumkit.

DEVELOPING 4 WAY INDEPENDENCE AND BALANCE

The human brain is like any other muscle in the body, if it isn't worked a certain way it won't improve in that way. Our brain stimulates muscle fibre, (which fibres and to what degree directly affects co-ordination, control and balance), by firing electrical impulses via synapses. The number of synapses designated to perform a task depends upon the **importance** of that task. The level of importance of a task is determined by the degree of **frequency, duration** and **intensity** of that task. The brain will increase synapse numbers over a period of time if the importance of the task is increased. This means it is possible to build new neural pathways or improve the efficiency of existing ones. The body via muscles, tendons, nerves etc. will also adapt to perform a physical task, depending upon its frequency, duration and intensity.

The exercise below is designed to improve balance and interaction between all limbs. Each limb interacts with every other limb as both leader (beats 1,2,3,4) and follower (all the '+'s'). Each new line (3 bars) introduces a new **lead** limb which is written in bold type at the beginning of each line. The other 3 limbs **follow** and are written in smaller type above the middle of the bar.

METHOD OF PRACTICE

The most difficult part of this exercise is memorising the order of limbs. Therefore, practice each line separately before attempting to join two or more together.

This is a 12 bar exercise, therefore only count each new repetition e.g. The first time through, all 12 bars are counted;

The second time through, all 12 bars are counted;

Try the exercise using double strokes and paradiddles instead of single strokes.

38.

OPEN HI-HAT EXERCISES

Open hi-hats are used to accentuate a particular beat or beats within a groove and can be added to any hi-hat hit.
The examples below introduce an open hi-hat(s) to different positions within the bar.

 **39.**

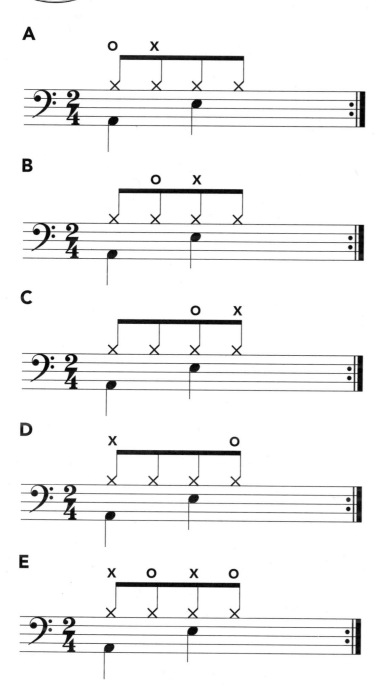

All the following grooves incorporate open hi-hat.

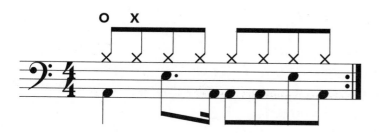

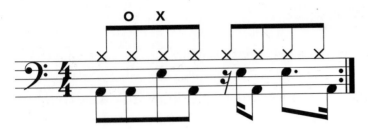

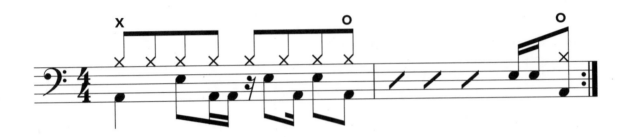

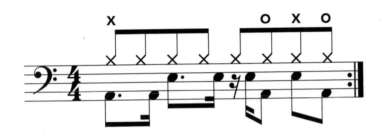

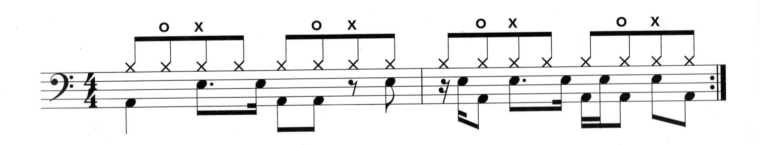

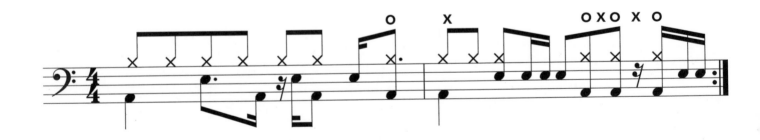

- Try adding open hi-hats to other patterns.
- Try adding open hi-hats to triplet hi-hat patterns.
- Try adding open hi-hats to sixteenth note hi-hat patterns.

GHOST NOTES

A ghost note is a note which is played as softly as possible.

All unaccented snare beats are 'ghosted' in the following examples.

Try playing the accented snares as **rimshots**. A rimshot is achieved by hitting the head (somewhere near the middle) and the hoop (at a point near the halfway mark of the stick) simultaneously.

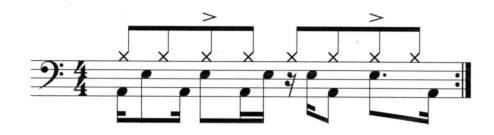

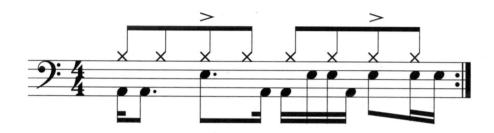

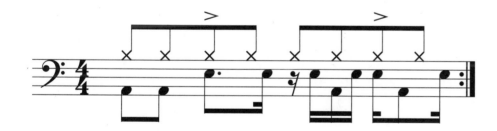

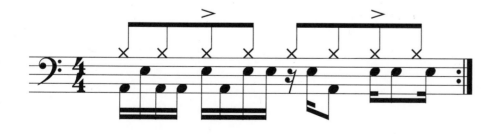

SOLO 29

40.

Apply ghosting technique to other patterns. Accented snare beats are most commonly '2' and '4' (backbeat).

FILL-INS FEATURING BASS DRUM

The lowest frequency on a drumkit is produced by the bass drum. The extra depth and impact of the bass drum sound can be utilised in the creation of drum fills.

The examples which follow introduce a basic pattern incorporating both hands and bass drum. Each basic pattern is followed by 2 or 3 variations, which explore different sound source and or rhythmic possibilities, and or combine the basic pattern with other patterns.

 **41.0**

 **41.1**

176

 **42.0**

 **42.1**

 **43.0**

43.1

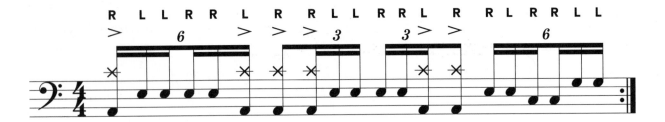

Here are some miscellaneous fills featuring bass drum.

THE TIE

A tie is a curved line joining two or more notes of the same pitch, where the second note(s) is not played , but its value added to that of the first note.

ADVANCED SYNCOPATION

Drummers, unlike most instrumentalists, cannot hold a note for a specific length of time. Therefore, some rhythmic figures can sound identical when played on a drumkit, yet be notated differently. The following examples show 3 ways of notating identically sounding rhythmic figures.

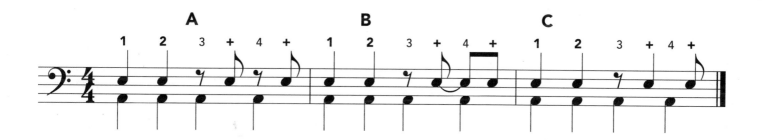

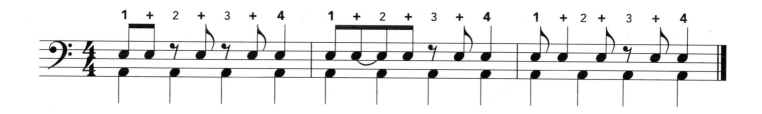

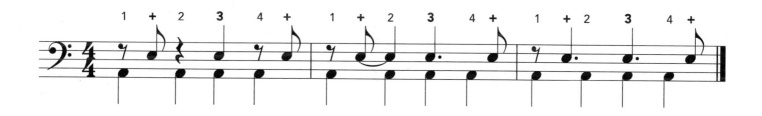

Examples 45.0 and 45.1 are 16 bar syncopated reading exercises. It is very important to count through these exercises as written. Reading syncopation is difficult and takes time. Working out a bar or a few bars at a time and then progressing to the next section works effectively.

SIGHT READING EXERCISE 26

45.0

SIGHT READING EXERCISE 27

 **45.1**

LINEAR PATTERNS

Strictly speaking, a linear pattern, as the name suggests, is any pattern whose individual voices never appear in unison. In real terms, the name is used on patterns which predominantly adhere to the above. Linear patterns are usually very syncopated and occur most often in Funk and Jazz Fusion music.

One way to create a linear pattern:

1) Select a sticking based upon the paradiddle or any of its inversions.

2) Create a bass drum rhythm based upon a bass guitar part, or just select a rhythm of interest.

3) Remove all hi-hat and snare beats which occur in unison with the bass drum rhythm.

4) Accent 1-3 snare beats, ghosting the remaining unaccented snare hits. Play accented snares as rimshots.

Here is a sticking pattern made up of the paradiddle and an inversion. (beat 6 becomes beat 1).

Paradiddle   **Inversion**

Here is a bass drum rhythm.

Here is the composite pattern.

The final linear pattern featuring snare accents on beats 2 and 4.

 **46.**

More Linear Patterns

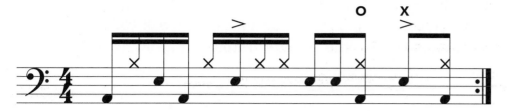

Swung Interpretation

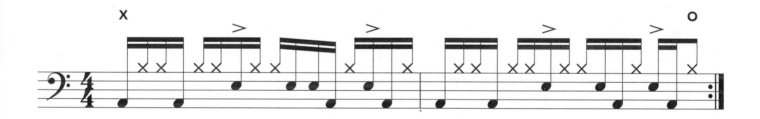

CD 2 47.

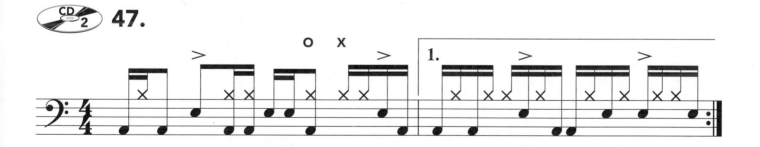

CREATING A DRUM PART

The groove below features a notated bass guitar part and a simple rock beat. The drum pattern uses an alternating kick and snare on the quarter notes and a simple eighth note hi-hat pattern.

 **48.0**

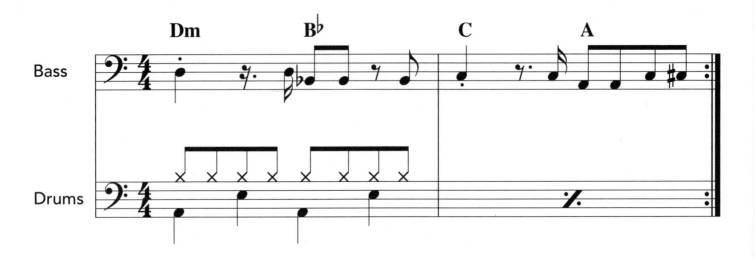

Music derives its interest from the application of **tension** and **release**.

Tension is created rhythmically through the use of **offbeats**. Using more offbeats creates greater rhythmic tension and greater **forward motion**.

The beat used in example 48.0 is **rhythmically resolved** as the rhythmic emphasis (created by the kick and snare rhythm) is on all the **onbeats** (beats 1,2,3,4).

The amount of forward motion used in a groove depends upon the music and the music style (e.g. Fusion grooves generally contain more forward motion than Rock grooves), the other musicians involved, and the personal choice of the drummer.

This example contains greater forward motion through the use of kick on beats '3+' and '4+" (both bars) and the open hi-hats on the same beats of bar 2.

 **48.1**

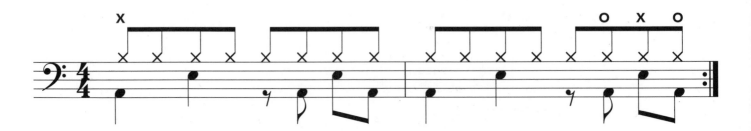

Different parts of the drumkit (voices, sound sources) can have a greater or lesser effect on the degree of forward motion e.g. shifting a snare accent to an offbeat has a more powerful impact than accenting an offbeat hi-hat.

The example below contains an accented offbeat snare hit in bar 2. Listen to the effect it has on the overall 'feel' of the music.

 **49.0**

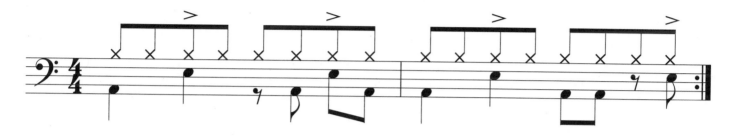

Adding ghost notes (explained in detail on page 173) is an excellent way to subtly create more forward motion without cluttering the music.

All unaccented snare hits are ghosted in the example below.

 **49.1**

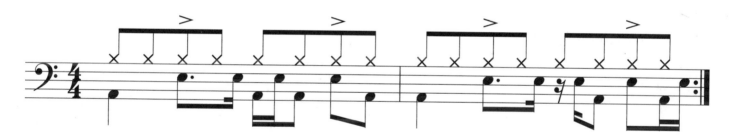

Another concept to be aware of when creating a groove is that of **unison** and **counterpoint**. Using the interaction of bass guitar and drums, unison is where the rhythm of the bass guitar is repeated in the drum pattern. The previous 4 examples all contained a bass drum rhythm which was in unison with the bass guitar.

The example below introduces counterpoint in the bass drum line on beats '1+', '2e', '4e' and '4a' in the second bar.

 **49.2**

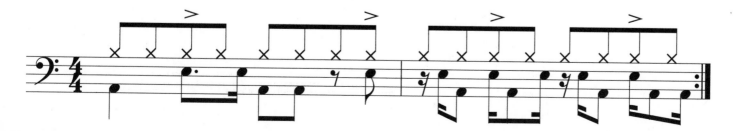

This example features a syncopated hi-hat pattern. The bass drum plays a unison line with the bass guitar. The combination of these elements gives the groove a 'funky feel'.

 **50.0**

Linear patterns tend to be very syncopated and hence contain a greater degree of forward motion.

 **50.1**

Musicality is a combination of technical execution, stylistic accuracy, musical appropriateness and rhythmic and sound source choices. Some of the greatest ever drum grooves only sound great because of when and where they were played. They 'lifted' the music to another level. This should be the goal of all drummers.

A few things to keep in mind:
- Often less is more.
- All music styles contain unique rhythmic nuances (feel) and place differing degrees of importance on different sound sources. The only way to play any style convincingly is to **listen** to as much material as possible as often as possible.

POLYRHYTHMS

Polyrhythmic literally means 'many rhythms'. A polyrhythm occurs when two or more rhythmic pulses are played simultaneously.

There are 2 basic ways to create a polyrhythm:

1) Any even note grouping (½, ¼, ⅛, ⅟₁₆ or ⅟₃₂ notes) sub**divided by an even number.**

2) Any odd note grouping (triplets, groups of 5,7,9,11 etc.) sub**divided by an even number.**

There are 3 ways to 'subdivide':

1) Sticking

2) Sound Source

3) Accent

or a combination of the above.

The amount a particular note grouping is subdivided by, distinguishes different polyrhythms e.g.

These eighth notes have been subdivided by 3 through the use of accents. This is a 3 against 8 polyrhythm. All **3 against 8** polyrhythms take 3 bars to complete one **cycle**. (3 times through the 8 pulse or 8 times through the 3 pulse). This formula is the same for all polyrhythms.

The fill-ins below are all 3 against 16 polyrhythms over one bar. The subdivisions of 3 have been created by sticking and or sound source selection. Because these polyrhythms do not evenly resolve over one bar, it is necessary to change the subdivision pattern at the end of the bar e.g. In this case the sticking pattern of the last two sixteenth notes has been changed:

becomes

Finishing a fill with the left hand facilitates an easier return to the beat.

Polyrhythms become more difficult as the duration held increases. Try these 2 bar 3 against 8 polyrhythms.

Here are the complete cycles of the 3 against 8 polyrhythms created with the sticking **R L L** and **R R L**. Fluency over polyrhythms relies upon the ability to distinguish both the polyrhythm and the pulse dictated by the time signature, simultaneously. In this case, the $\frac{4}{4}$ time signature is accentuated by the quarter note bass drum pulse.

 **51.0**

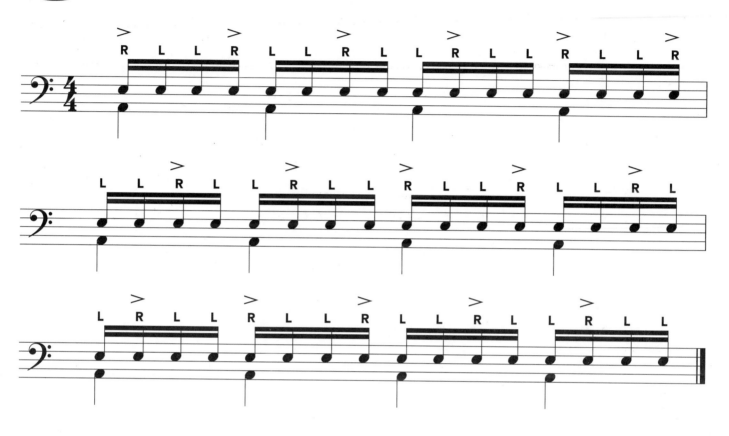

 **51.1**

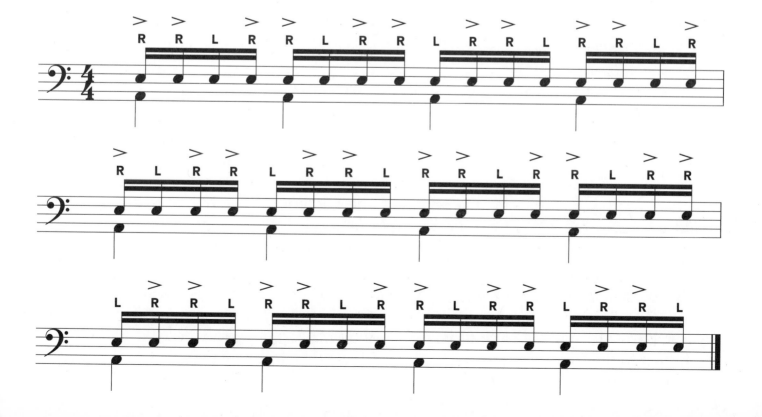

SECTION 8

ADVANCED INDEPENDENCE - CONCEPT 1

There are 16 possible rhythmic variations over 1 beat using quarter notes, eighth notes, sixteenth notes, quarter, eighth and sixteenth note rests and the dot.

Using these 16 rhythms as the basis for practice ideas allows us to develop the technical facility necessary to play countless ideas whilst practicing small numbers of exercises.

e.g. Using one limb and one sound source, it is possible to play 65,536 different rhythms in $\frac{4}{4}$ time, by joining the sixteen rhythmic possibilities together in different ways.

$$\frac{4}{4} \quad 16 \quad \times \quad 16 \quad \times \quad 16 \quad \times \quad 16 \quad = 65,536$$

Beat 1   Beat 2   Beat 3   Beat 4

If another limb was factored in the equation, the number of possible rhythmic variations would be 4,294,967,296. There are still two or more limbs, countless sound sources, accent possibilities, sticking possibilities etc. The possibilities are infinite.

Two points are important here:

1) It is possible to play something totally unique. Something that has never before been played. Certainly each persons unique physiology, emotional make up and choice of ideas in particular musical settings **will** make their playing unique.

2) Understanding rhythmic possibilities and knowing how to use them is the foundation for infinite exploration of your own ideas.

Musical choices are greatly expanded by mastering the ability to **improvise** with one or more limbs whilst playing various **ostinatos** (repetitive patterns). This process is called **independence**. The ostinatos will vary depending upon the musical style. e.g. playing in a rock style often requires independence with kick or snare whilst playing a repetitive eighth note hi-hat pattern. The kick and or snare play varied rhythms based upon the bass guitar line primarily and or the chordal and melodic instrument parts.

A useful exercise for developing bass drum independence in the rock style would be; bass drum plays each of the 16 rhythmic variations with the following ostinato.

Here are the remaining 15 rhythmic variations.

 **52.**

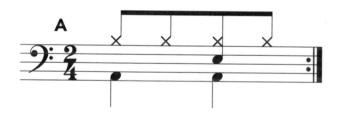

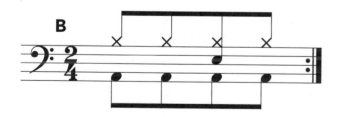

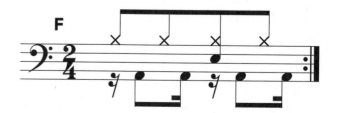

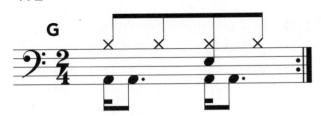

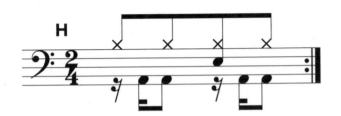

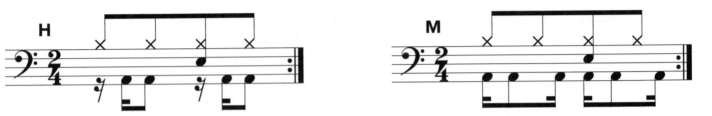

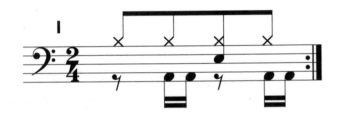

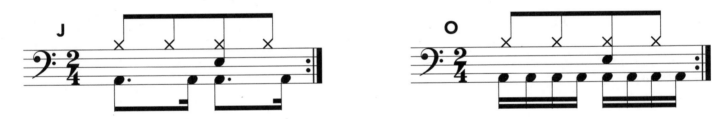

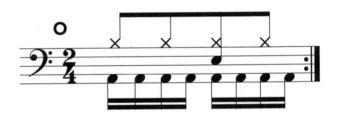

SOLO 30

This 12 bar solo requires the independence skills developed from the study of material on the previous page.

53.

The patterns on the following page are designed to develop snare drum independence with the following ostinato.

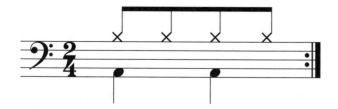

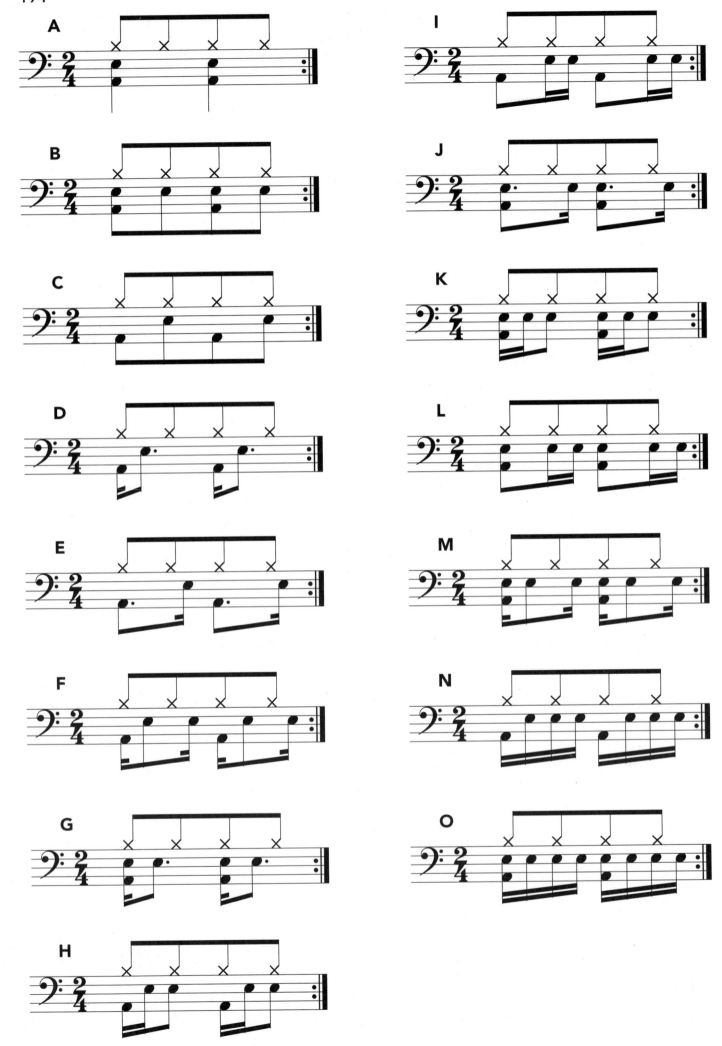

SOLO 31

This 12 bar solo requires the independence skills developed from the study of material on the previous page.

 **54.**

The patterns below feature bass drum rhythms created via the rhythmic possibilities concept, with the snare drum filling in the sixteenth note 'gaps'.

55.

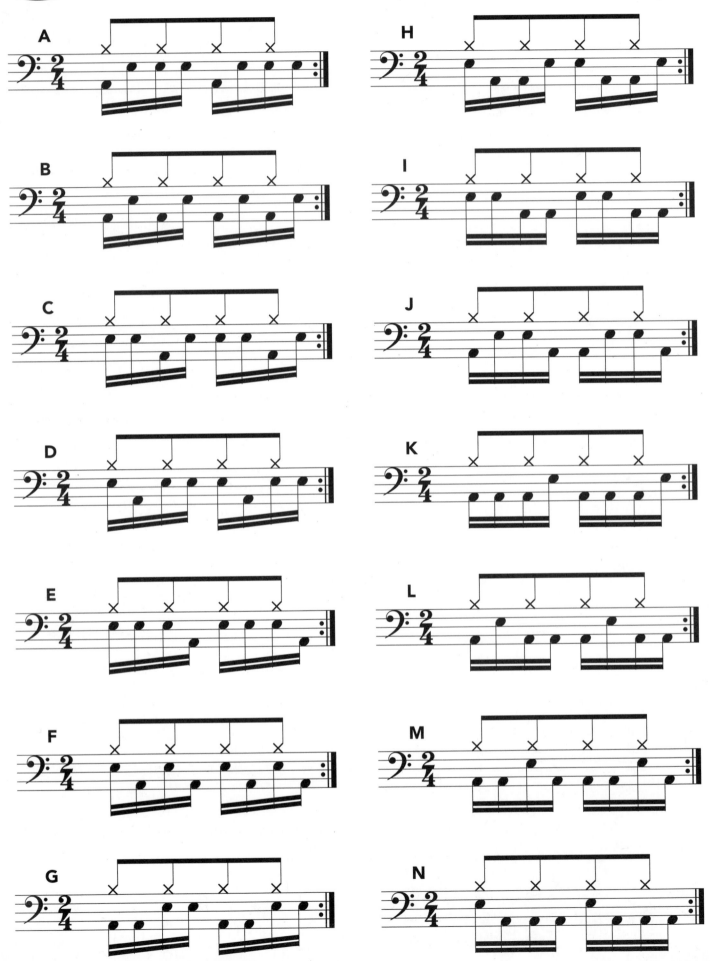

SOLO 32

This 12 bar solo requires the independence skills developed from the study of material on the previous pages.

56.

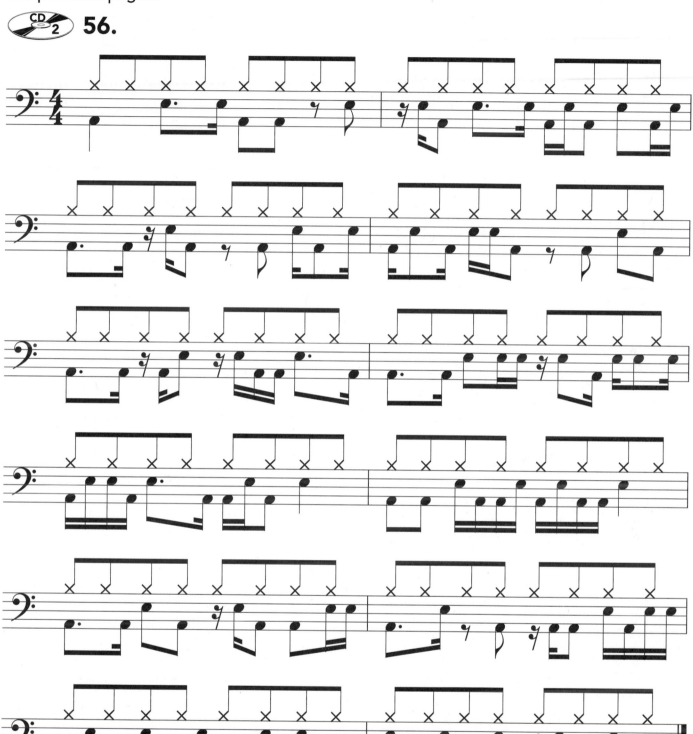

ACCENT STUDIES

The patterns on the following page use the rhythmic possibilities concept to dictate the position of accented notes with the following ostinato.

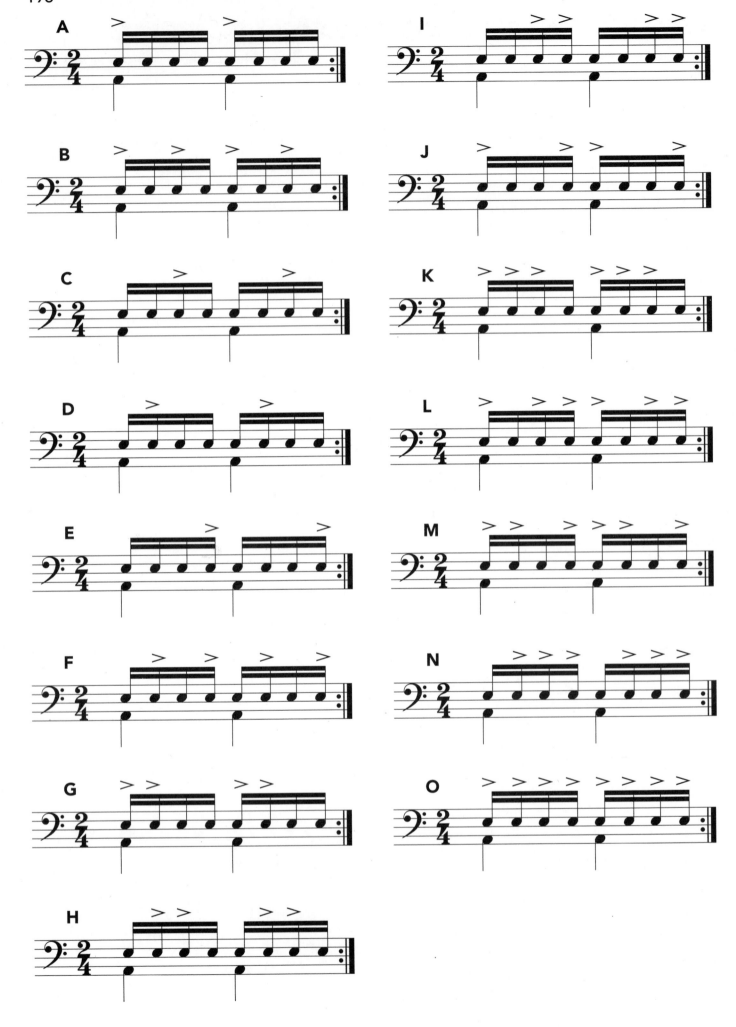

ADVANCED INDEPENDENCE CONCEPT 2 - TRIPLETS

There are 8 possible rhythmic variations over 1 beat using quarter notes, eighth note triplets, quarter note rests and eighth note triplet rests.

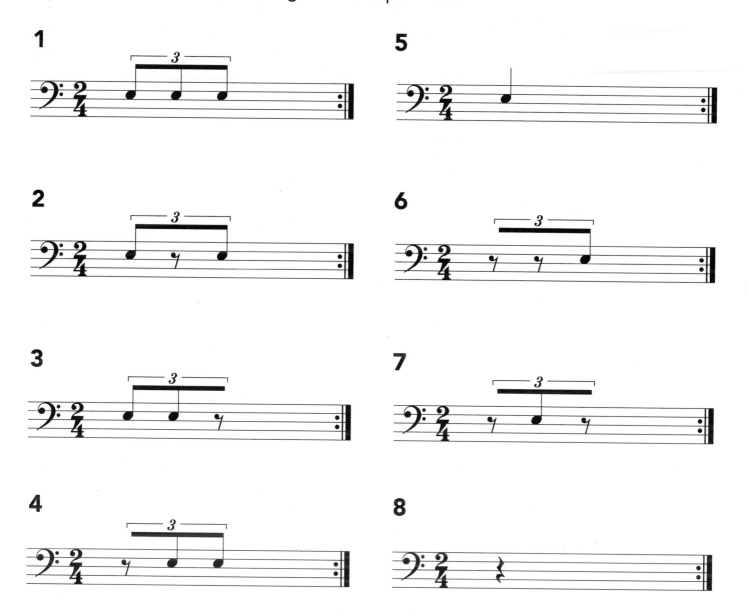

Using the same principle outlined on pages 190 and 191, the following patterns are designed to develop bass drum independence with the following ostinato:

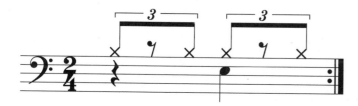

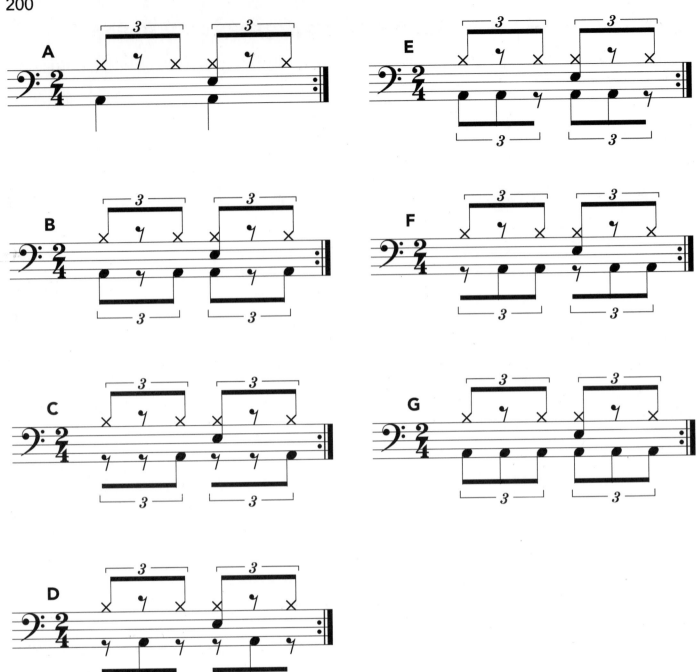

The patterns below are designed to develop snare drum independence with the following ostinato:

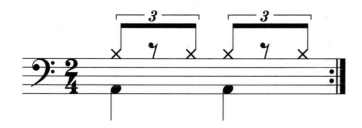

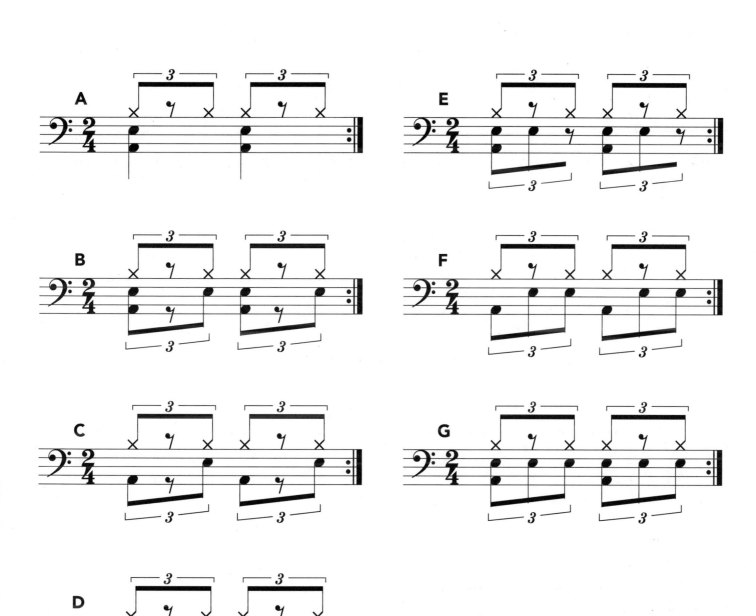

TRIPLET ACCENT STUDIES

The patterns below use the rhythmic possibilities concept to dictate the position of accented notes with the following ostinato:

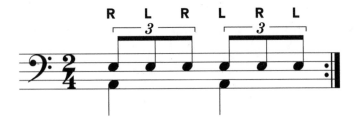

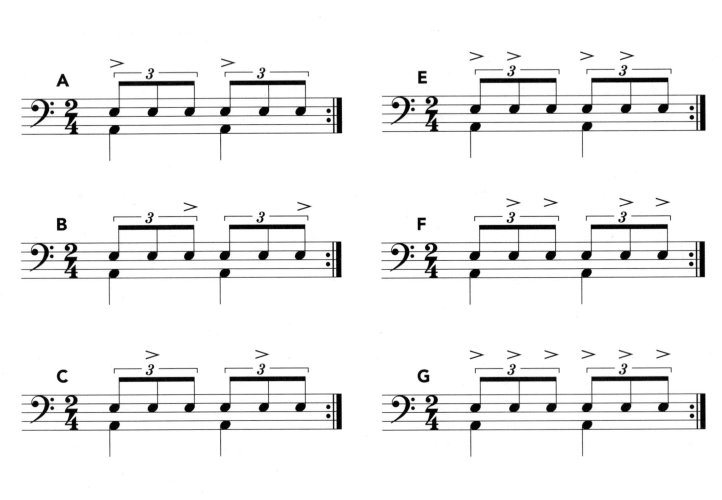

COMBINATION SIGHT READING EXERCISES

The following 3 sight reading exercises feature combinations of various rhythmic figures. Each exercise is highly syncopated and requires a sound understanding of previous sight reading material.

New rhythmic figures are added to successive exercises.

It may be necessary to break each exercise into smaller digestible pieces e.g. - learn each bar individually, learn combination of 2,4 and 8 bar phrases, before attempting the entire 16 bars.

SIGHT READING EXERCISE 28

CD 2 57.

SIGHT READING EXERCISE 29

 **58.**

SIGHT READING EXERCISE 30

59.

COMBINATION TRIPLET SIGHT READING EXERCISE

The following sight reading exercise features combinations of various triplet rhythmic figures.

SIGHT READING EXERCISE 31

60.

ADVANCED INDEPENDENCE CONCEPT 3

The combination sight reading exercises can be used to further develop co-ordination and independence in the following way:

1) Choose an ostinato.

2) Choose the limb and voice requiring independence.

3) The chosen limb from step 2 plays the sight reading exercise whilst the appropriate limbs simultaneously play the ostinato chosen at step 1.

HERE IS AN EXAMPLE OF THE PROCESS:

STEP 1 - Ostinato pattern:

STEP 2 - Right foot, Bass Drum

STEP 3 - Here is an example of step 3, using the first 4 bars of the combination sight reading exercise on page 203.

 **61.0**

The advanced independence concept 3 explained previously, can also be used in conjunction with the triplet combination sight reading exercise on page 206.
Here is an example of that process:

STEP 1 - Ostinato pattern

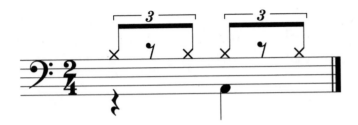

STEP 2 - Left hand, sidestick

STEP 3 - Here is an example of step 3, using the first 4 bars of the triplet combination sight reading exercise.

 **61.1**

OSTINATO PATTERNS

Here are some suggested ostinato patterns which can be used with advanced concepts 1, 2 and 3. The suggested limb and voice requiring independence (step 2 on page 207) is listed with each ostinato.

The ostinatos are split into 2 categories:

1) **STRAIGHT INTERPRETATION** - limb requiring independence plays:
    (i) Rhythmic possibilities on page 190.
    (ii) Sight reading exercises on pages 203 - 205.

2) **TRIPLET INTERPRETATION** - limb requiring independence plays:
    (i) Rhythmic possibilities on page 199.
    (ii) Sight reading exercise on page 206, swung interpretation of sight reading exercises on pages 180 and 181.

STRAIGHT INTERPRETATION

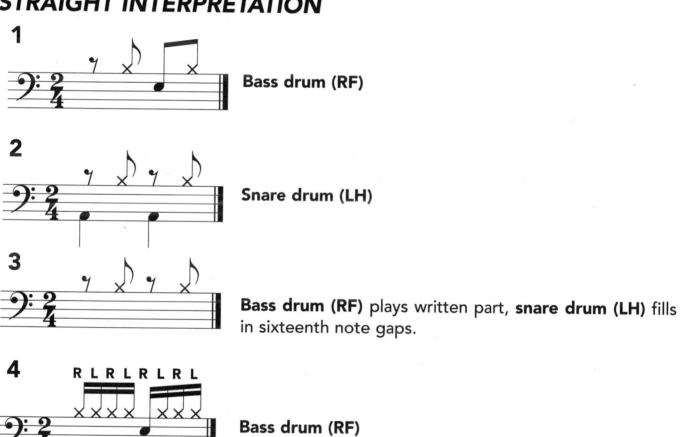

1 Bass drum (RF)

2 Snare drum (LH)

3 Bass drum (RF) plays written part, snare drum (LH) fills in sixteenth note gaps.

4 Bass drum (RF)

5 Snare drum (RH or LH)

6 Bass drum (RF) plays written part, snare drum (LH) fills in sixteenth note gaps.

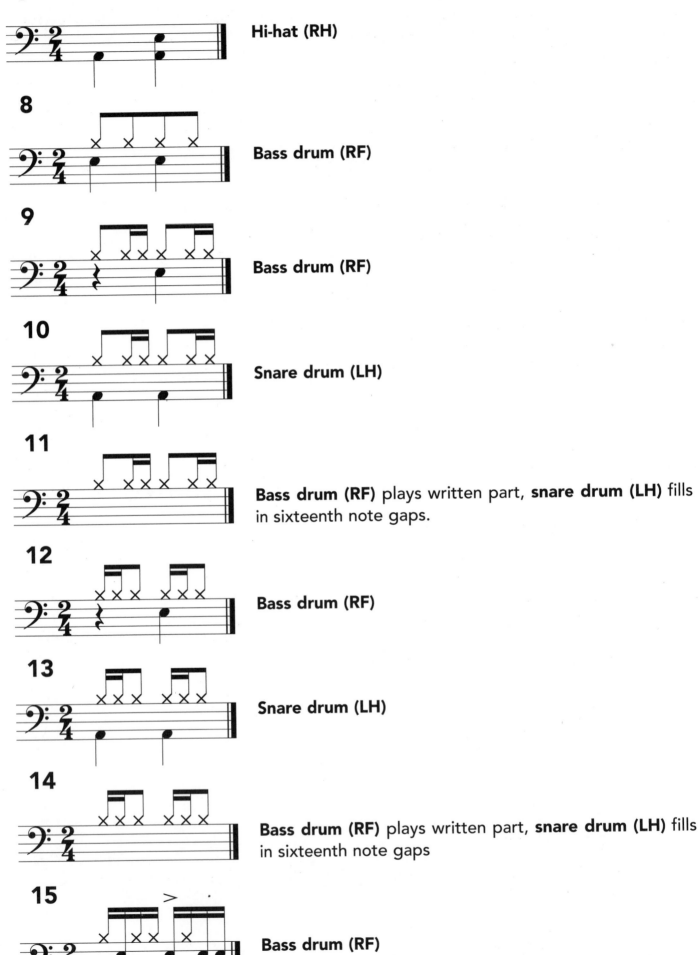

7
Hi-hat (RH)

8
Bass drum (RF)

9
Bass drum (RF)

10
Snare drum (LH)

11
Bass drum (RF) plays written part, **snare drum (LH)** fills in sixteenth note gaps.

12
Bass drum (RF)

13
Snare drum (LH)

14
Bass drum (RF) plays written part, **snare drum (LH)** fills in sixteenth note gaps

15
Bass drum (RF)

16

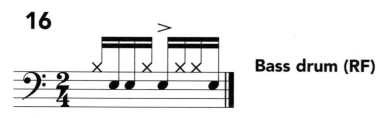

Bass drum (RF)

Note:
RH= Right Hand   **LH**=Left Hand   **RF**=Right Foot

OSTINATO PATTERNS - TRIPLET INTERPRETATION

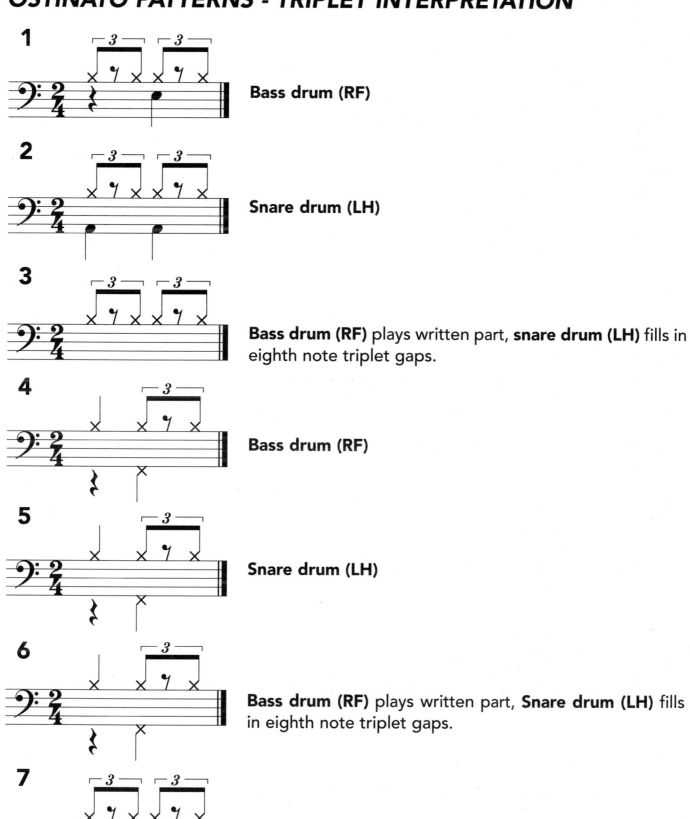

1

Bass drum (RF)

2

Snare drum (LH)

3

Bass drum (RF) plays written part, **snare drum (LH)** fills in eighth note triplet gaps.

4

Bass drum (RF)

5

Snare drum (LH)

6

Bass drum (RF) plays written part, **Snare drum (LH)** fills in eighth note triplet gaps.

7

Sidestick (LH)

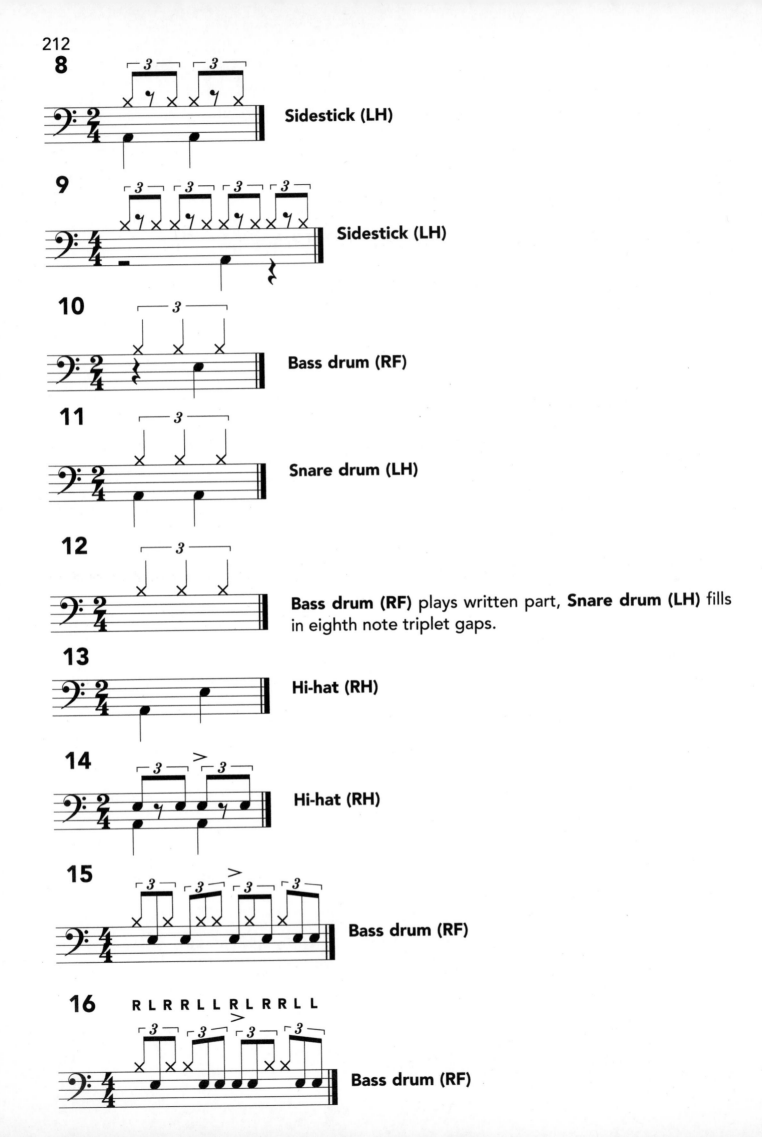

-Create your own ostinatos.

-Develop independence with the limb of your choice.

-Try adding a foot closed hi-hat pattern to each ostinato e.g.

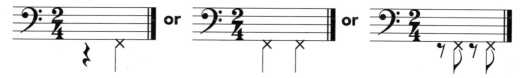

-Remember to count.

JAZZ INDEPENDENCE

Jazz independence refers to the ability to co-ordinate snare and or bass drum beats independently to that of the swing ride cymbal pattern. Most 'comping' (phrasing with snare and or bass drum) rhythms are derived from eighth note triplets and eighth note triplet rests. In $\frac{4}{4}$ time, there are 390,625 rhythmic possibilities for snare and or bass drum using eighth note triplets and eighth note triplet rests. The method below is designed to develop comping independence with a swing ride pattern, using the fewest possible exercises.

There are 16 independence exercises (combinations of snare and or bass drum over 4 events).

1.	S	S	S	S		**5.**	S	S	S	B		**9.**	S	B	S	S		**13.**	S	S	B	B
2.	B	B	B	B		**6.**	B	B	B	S		**10**	B	S	B	B		**14.**	B	B	S	S
3.	B	S	B	S		**7.**	S	B	B	B		**11.**	S	S	B	S		**15.**	S	B	B	S
4.	S	B	S	B		**8.**	B	S	S	S		**12.**	B	B	S	B		**16.**	B	S	S	B

Note: S = Snare Drum   B = Bass Drum

 **62.**

There are 7 **comping rhythms**.

214

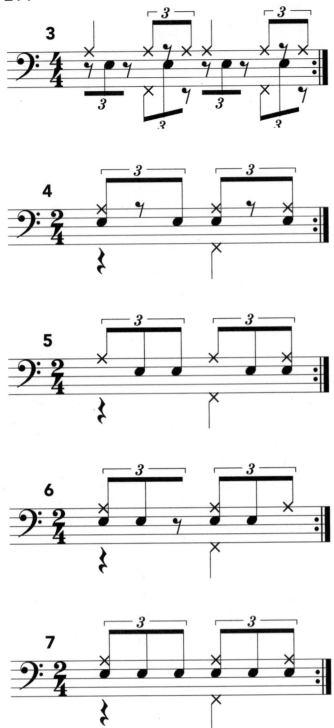

Note: Comping rhythms 1-6 are written using independence exercise 1. Comping rhythm 7 is expanded upon on page 216.

Play the 16 independence exercises with the first 6 comping rhythms e.g.

Comping rhythm **1** with independence exercise **5**.

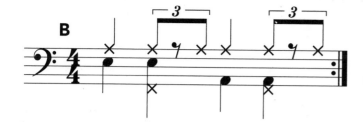

Comping rhythm **1** with independence exercise **13**.

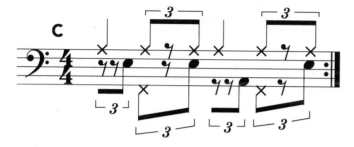

Comping rhythm **2** with independence exercise **11**.

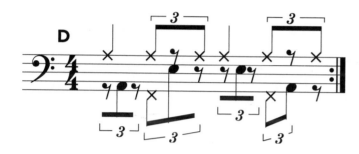

Comping rhythm **3** with independence exercise **16**.

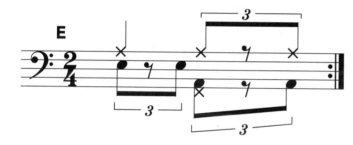

Comping rhythm **4** with independence exercise **13**.

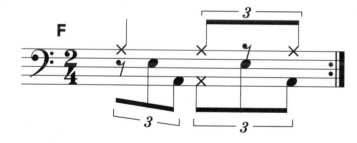

Comping rhythm **5** with independence exercise **4**.

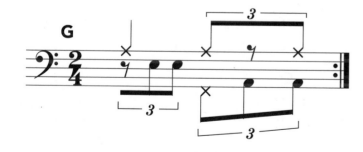

Comping rhythm **5** with independence exercise **13**.

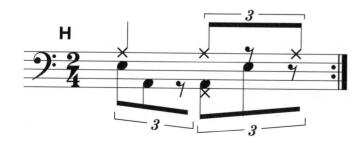

Comping rhythm **6** with independence exercise **15**.

Here are some independence exercises for comping rhythm 7.

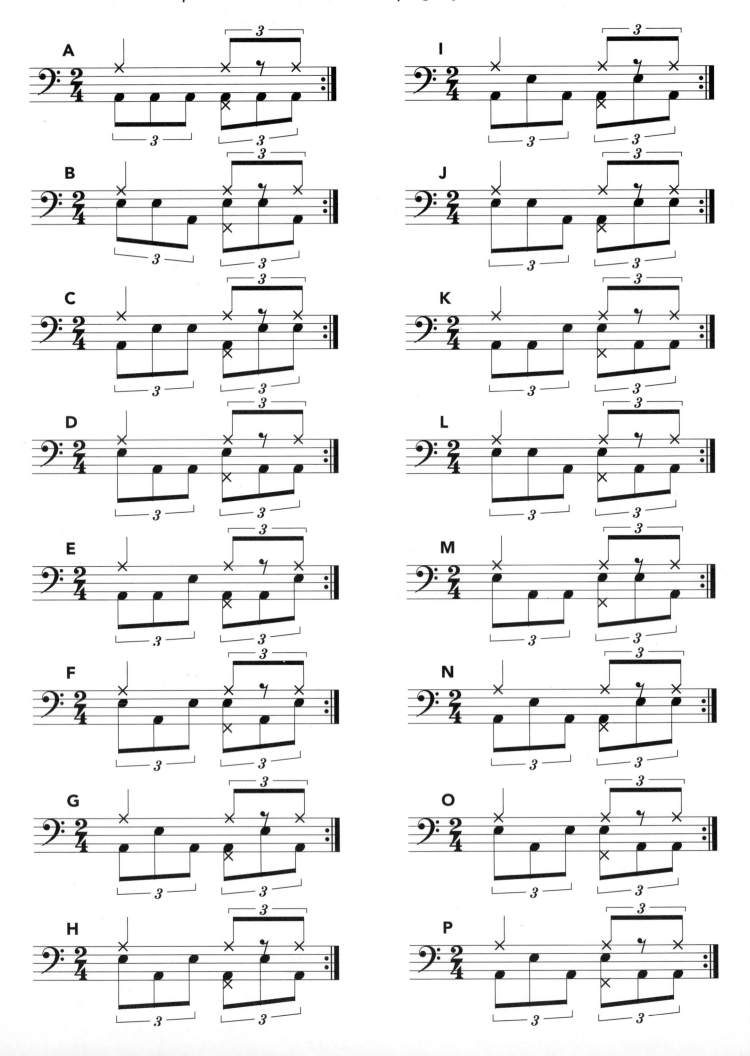

SECTION 9

SOLO SUPPLEMENT   *SOLO 33*

 63.   Funky Mama

INTRO FILL

An intro fill is only played at the beginning of a piece of music and not upon subsequent repeats. This solo features an intro fill.

ANTICIPATION

Anticipation is where the downbeat is anticipated by the preceding offbeat. This solo features an anticipation of beat 1 by the preceding offbeat triplet ('4 a') in bars 5 and 7.

SOLO 34

64. Highway 69

Repeat and Fade

SOLO 35

65.   **Bourbon St. Blues**

Ritard

SOLO 36

 66. **Reggae 2 Drop**

snare wires off

SOLO 37

67. **Jazz 'n' It**

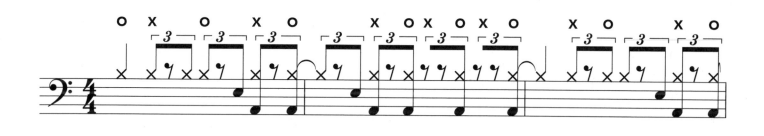

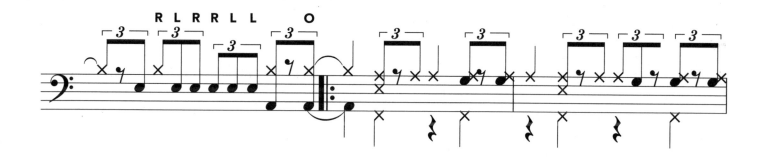

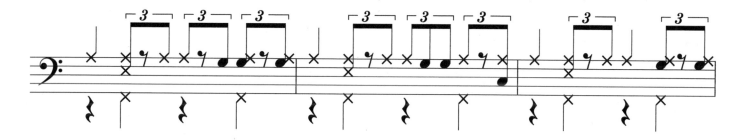

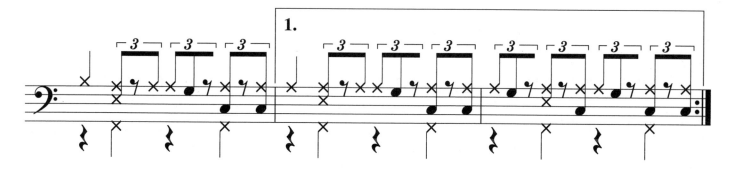

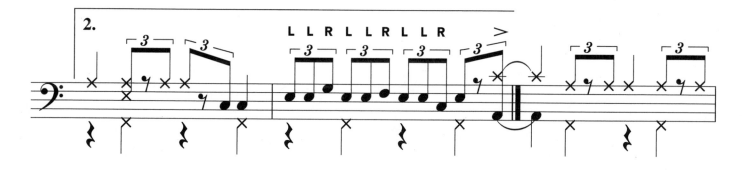